Taking Flight

The St. Louis Cardinals and the
Building of Baseball's Best Franchise

ROB RAINS

TRIUMPH
B O O K S

The Library of Congress Cataloging-in-Publication Data
Names: Rains, Rob.
Title: Taking flight : the St. Louis Cardinals and the building of baseball's best franchise / Rob Rains.
Description: Chicago, Illinois : Triumph Books, 2016.
Identifiers: LCCN 2015039966 | ISBN 9781629370859 (hardback)
Subjects: LCSH: St. Louis Cardinals (Baseball team) | BISAC: SPORTS & RECREATION / Baseball / General. | TRAVEL / United States / Midwest / West / North Central (IA, KS, MN, MO, ND, NE, SD).
Classification: LCC GV875.S74 R36 2016 | DDC 796.357/640977866—dc23 LC record available at http://lccn.loc.gov/2015039966

This book is available in quantity at special discounts for your group or organization. For further information, contact:

Triumph Books LLC
814 N. Franklin
Chicago, Illinois 60610
www.triumphbooks.com

Printed in United States of America
ISBN: 978-1-62937-085-9
Page production by Amy Carter

This book is dedicated to all of the men who worked so tirelessly over the years as scouts, minor-league managers, coaches, and instructors to sign and develop players who would go on to star with the St. Louis Cardinals, most notably George Kissell, Dave Ricketts, Hub Kittle, Bo Milliken, and Fred McAlister, all of whom definitely bled Cardinals red.

CONTENTS

FOREWORD

AS MUCH AS BASEBALL HAS CHANGED OVER THE YEARS, THERE IS AT least one fact which is the same now as it was 50 years ago: the teams which have the most success are almost always the ones which have done the best job of scouting, drafting, and developing their own players.

This is especially true with the St. Louis Cardinals.

The Cardinals won a major-league-best 100 games in the regular season in 2015, and they did it despite having their top pitcher, their No. 3 hitter, and their regular first baseman on the disabled list for much of the season.

The Cardinals' success was due in large part to the contributions they received from players coming up from the minor leagues who filled in for Adam Wainwright, Matt Holliday, and Matt Adams. I don't think the Cardinals would have won 100 games without players such as Stephen Piscotty, Randal Grichuk, and Tommy Pham doing what they did, and their performance was a testimony to the work that goes on in their minor-league system.

The team went into the postseason with 15 players on its 25-man roster who were homegrown players—and that total did not include Wainwright or Grichuk, both of whom were acquired in trades when they were still minor-leaguers. It also didn't include two more homegrown players, Adams and Carlos Martinez, who would have been on the roster had they been healthy.

Only four of those players—Michael Wacha, Lance Lynn, Kolten Wong, and Piscotty—were acquired in the first round of the draft or with supplemental picks between the first and second rounds. And none of the four were selected higher than 19th overall.

Because of their recent success, the Cardinals rarely get picks in the top part of the draft. Since 2000, they have had only two picks higher than 18th overall, both times holding the 13th pick. To be able to have the success they have had since then—making the playoffs 12 times in 16 seasons—really is remarkable, even though the expansion of the playoffs has made it easier to get there than it used to be.

The draft was created in 1965 to try to level the baseball playing field and keep the teams with the most money from just going out and outspending other teams and signing the best prospects. It really has worked out pretty well, but one truth hasn't changed—luck still plays a big role in which of those prospects make it to the major leagues and which don't.

The increased use of computer analysis and statistics has changed the game and provided more information for teams making decisions about drafting players, signing free agents, or swinging trades. The teams which have had the most success in recent years, in my opinion, are the ones which have done the best job of incorporating the new-school philosophy with the old standard of having scouts in the field, watching and observing, and instructors and coaches working with the young players.

So much information is available now it really can be overwhelming. I went to one Cardinals game in 2015 and sat down before the game to read the notes and statistics—and kept reading between innings—and was still reading in the ninth inning. That is a lot of data to digest.

All of that statistical analysis is just one of the resources available to teams today. Another is the sheer number of coaches and instructors on each minor-league team. When I was running the Mets' farm system in the late 1960s and early 1970s, we had one manager for each of our six teams. We had one pitching coach for the entire minor-league system. And we had me. Now, every team has a manager, a hitting coach, a pitching coach, and a trainer, and they have roving instructors who go through the system spending time with each team.

How well the people who work for the Cardinals do those jobs is reflected by the success of the players who come through their system.

One fact which really can't be measured or discounted, however, is luck. Nothing proves that better than what happened when I was helping run the draft for the Mets in 1966, the second year of the draft.

Bing Devine and I were in charge, and we had the first overall pick. Oakland was picking second. We chose a high school catcher from California, Steve Chilcott, who really was an exciting young player. With the second pick, the A's took an outfielder from Arizona State—Reggie Jackson.

We had scouted Jackson and thought he was a good prospect, but we also had a major-league outfield at the time of Tommie Agee, Cleon Jones, and Ron Swoboda. We needed a catcher.

The 18-year-old Chilcott was hitting .290 and leading the

Florida State League in doubles when he dove back into second base one night and tore up his shoulder. This was also a time when players had to serve in the military, and he left the team to report to the Army after he had been out about two months.

He was crawling on his belly as part of an exercise during training and caught his shoulder on some barbed wire and tore the hell out of it again. When he came back from the service, he could throw adequately but he couldn't swing a bat. He hung around for a few years but his career was over before he turned 24.

There were 20 teams in the major leagues then, and after that draft, Bing told me to go around the room in New York and find out how many teams had Chilcott as the top player on their board, and how many had Jackson. The vote was 11 to nine. That's how close it was, but it didn't work out for us. When the Mets won the World Series three years later, in 1969, we didn't have a first- or second-round draft pick on our team.

There is no doubt a team has to be lucky to win, but you usually create that luck through hard work, attention to detail, and knowing how to motivate your players, and that starts in the minor leagues. The Cardinals do as good a job of that as anybody—and that's the biggest reason why they are the best franchise in baseball.

—*Whitey Herzog*

PROLOGUE

BRANCH RICKEY WAS FRUSTRATED.

Running the St. Louis Cardinals in the 1920s, Rickey had a keen eye for young baseball talent but he also had a limited budget. Whenever he or his top scout, Charley Barrett, found a minor-league player they liked, another team almost always topped the Cardinals' meager bid and ended up signing him.

On some occasions, after Rickey or Barrett saw a particular player, executives from that minor-league team—knowing the Cardinals could not offer much money—sent word to other teams that Rickey had shown interest. Even without seeing the player, rival clubs often offered more money than the Cardinals, basing their decision entirely on Rickey's opinion.

At that time, buying players from minor-league teams—which all operated independently—was the only way for major-league teams to acquire players.

Rickey knew there had to be a better way to stock his roster. What if, he asked owner Sam Breadon, we had our own minor-league clubs, which would develop players strictly for the Cardinals?

"I'll find the players somewhere," Rickey told Breadon. "I don't know where, but I have a lot of friends all around the country who know their baseball. I'll get them to look around their corner lots, their college diamonds, their semipro parks, and we'll eventually develop a farm system in our own business.

"We'll send those kids to our minor-league ballclubs and we'll grow and grow, until we get even with (John) McGraw and the (New York) Giants and the rest of them."

Commissioner Kennesaw Mountain Landis opposed the idea, believing it would threaten the success of minor-league teams, but Rickey was adamant in pursuing his plan. Flush with cash after the Cardinals sold the land where Robison Field stood to the St. Louis Public Schools and a transit company, moving back to Sportsman's Park as a tenant of the St. Louis Browns, Rickey bought shares in minor-league teams in Houston; Fort Smith, Arkansas; and Syracuse, New York.

The Cardinals' farm system had been born.

One of the ways Rickey found players to stock those minor-league teams was through tryout camps. In the summer of 1940, Rickey went to Rochester, New York, for a camp and about 400 would-be players showed up. One of them was a 19-year-old infielder named George Kissell.

Kissell was home for the summer from Ithaca College, where he would earn bachelor's and master's degrees in physical education and history. Kissell was helping work on the family farm in Evans Mills, New York, when he heard about the tryout camp and asked his father if he could go.

His father said no. There was work to be done on the farm.

Nobody will ever know if it was a case of divine intervention but the night before the tryout camp, it rained—making it too wet for the Kissells to work in the fields. Father and son got in the family car and drove to Rochester.

Kissell fielded five ground balls at shortstop and the next day was one of five or six players Rickey wanted to sign. He asked Kissell's father how much the trip to Rochester had cost in expenses. The answer was $19.80. Rickey handed over $20, telling him he could consider the 20 cents a signing bonus.

Nobody had any way of knowing then, of course, how many lives would change because of that event. Except for three years he spent in the Navy in World War II, and when he worked as a substitute teacher in the winter, Kissell never earned a paycheck from anybody other than the Cardinals.

He never had an at-bat or fielded a ball in the major leagues, nor did he ever serve as the Cardinals' manager, but there is little doubt no one man had as much influence over any organization from the 1940s through the next 60-plus years as Kissell did with the Cardinals. He became a player-manager at the age of 25 and was still in uniform, working with players, six decades later.

Especially when it came to developing "the Cardinal way," nobody was more influential than Kissell—who wrote the team's organization manual about how to practice fundamentals, about the importance of acting as a professional, and the necessity of concentrating on doing all of the little things right in order to be successful.

Even after his death from injuries suffered in a car accident in 2008, when he was 88 years old, Kissell's teachings live on today in the lessons and instructions he passed on to managers and coaches in the Cardinals' farm system.

Current players who are too young to have ever met Kissell

still know of him and go through the same drills and routines that he developed decades ago.

The players who came through the system and did know Kissell, however, never forgot him.

One of those young players was a rookie outfielder, drafted in the first round in 1979 out of a rural New York high school. Andy Van Slyke still remembers the first time Kissell spoke to his team.

"My first impression was I felt like a first-grader in a college lecture," Van Slyke said. "I never knew there was so much to the game of baseball. I just played it. He was the ultimate professor of the game. I didn't realize how much I didn't know about the game until I hung around George Kissell for the first three years of my minor-league career."

Kissell, as he had told countless players over the years, once told Van Slyke, "You never see a duck and a goose together."

"It took me about three weeks to figure out what it meant," Van Slyke said. "George had a way of making you think. That's what great teachers do. They don't program you to spit back information. They program you to think.

"More than anything else he taught me the wisdom of the game. He taught me to be wise about how to play the game. He is the only coach I've ever come around who helped you gain instincts. He had a gift. He matched philosophy with fundamentals in a way nobody else has ever done."

Seventy-five years after he joined the Cardinals, playing third base for the Hamilton Red Wings in an Ontario Class D league and earning $75 a month, Kissell became a member of the second class of inductees in the Cardinals Hall of Fame in August of 2015.

The honor was certainly appropriate, not only for what

Kissell did as an individual, but for what he represented and left behind in the organization.

Mike Shildt, now the manager of the Cardinals' Triple A team in Memphis, is one of those trying to honor and respect Kissell's legacy by the way he goes about his job.

"His wake is enormous, powerful, strong, and the reason is because, first of all, he was a straight shooter," Shildt said. "He was fundamental with everything he did. It made sense. It was practical. It was fair and it was honest. Importantly, it was based on the best interests of that player and the Cardinals organization. That's a legacy that is very impressive.

"We appreciate and understand how George had such a big part, and how he impressed upon people to care more about the organization than about themselves."

One of the lasting images Shildt has of Kissell was from a day early in spring training in 2008. Shildt had been put in charge of planning that spring training for the first time, and one of the people he sought out for advice was Kissell.

"I told George, 'We're not going to change anything. We're going to keep everything the same,'" Shildt said. "He wagged his finger in my face and said, 'You better do something. You better make it better.'"

For everybody in the organization, including players, managers, coaches, instructors, scouts, and administrators, that is still the focus of their jobs. They believe their sole objective is to do their jobs better than anybody else. That dedication and commitment has led to the construction and continued success of one of baseball's crown jewels, a franchise with 11 World Series championships and dozens of Hall of Famers.

This is their story.

1   JOHN MOZELIAK

THE COLORADO ROCKIES WERE JUST BEGINNING THEIR INAUGURAL season in 1993 when John Mozeliak answered a phone call from a friend who had gone to work as the team's video coordinator.

Jay Darnell had coached Mozeliak in American Legion ball for three years in Boulder, Colorado. He was calling to see if Mozeliak, who had graduated about a year earlier from the University of Colorado with a business degree, would be interested in becoming one of the Rockies' batting-practice pitchers.

Mozeliak had the only real qualification that mattered to the team—he threw left-handed.

At the time, Mozeliak said, "I was still trying to decide where I was going and what I might do. It started with a very simple phone call."

Mozeliak was soon throwing BP to Andres Galaragga, Dante Bichette, and the rest of the Rockies, and, gradually, found himself getting more involved in other assignments in the organization.

"It was something I didn't think would necessarily lead to a career," Mozeliak said. "But I was getting exposure to different elements of the baseball operations department. I started to realize that maybe I could help contribute to the department along the way. The one I was most interested in at the time was scouting because your playing background did not necessarily impede you from having success."

Mozeliak worked with Rockies general manager Bob Gebhard and assistant GM Walt Jocketty for more than two years.

In 1994, Jocketty was hired as the general manager of the Cardinals, and he offered Mozeliak a chance to move to St. Louis and work as an assistant in the scouting department.

"Before I accepted the job with Walt, what I wanted to know was that he would allow me to learn more about how decision-making worked in baseball," Mozeliak said. "I didn't want to just come in and help with the infrastructure, software, or the computer system, and in a year or two find myself going nowhere.

"That was the trade-off of me coming to the Cardinals."

It turned out Mozeliak didn't need to worry about "going nowhere." He steadily rose through a variety of jobs in the front office, becoming assistant GM to Jocketty in 2003.

"I was very fortunate to work with a lot of people who gave me opportunities," he said. "Getting exposure to a lot of different elements of the organization, that all helps define me today."

Mozeliak worked as assistant scouting director, scouting director, and director of baseball operations prior to his promotion to assistant GM.

That was the same year Cardinals chairman William DeWitt Jr., the head of a group which agreed to purchase the Cardinals from Anheuser-Busch in 1995, hired a young business executive, Jeff Luhnow, to fill a new position, vice president of baseball development.

"Mr. DeWitt made a conscious effort to redirect the organization and take a more analytical approach, ramping up the scouting department," Mozeliak said. "In turn we were able to have success in the draft, not only at the top but throughout the draft with a sophisticated approach of using scouts and statistics in a joint effort."

The change was not entirely smooth, however, with different factions—the analytics side and the baseball side—often at odds with each other. One of Mozeliak's jobs was to be a buffer between the two sides, but by the end of the 2007 season, DeWitt knew he could not tolerate the acrimony in the front office any longer. Jocketty was dismissed, and a month later, the 38-year-old Mozeliak was named the 12th general manager in franchise history.

It has been under Mozeliak's leadership that the Cardinals have continued to emphasize the blend of analytics, scouting, and player development as a means to achieving success at both the major-league and minor-league level.

"For our major-league success we have to have four strong pillars and we typically define them as international, the amateur draft, player development, and our baseball development group," Mozeliak said. "If those four legs are strong, the major-league team will be as well."

The Cardinals were perhaps at the forefront, and certainly had more success than other teams, in figuring out the proper way to blend the old-school and new-school approaches to analyzing data and player evaluations, on both the amateur and professional side.

"The simple way to think about it is we were just trying to increase our odds for success," Mozeliak said. "Ultimately the more we dove into this and took a more analytical approach we realized we were just strengthening our own decisions or having more positive outcomes.

"It's always fluid because you are always learning and things change, but I will say from just a disciplinary standpoint we know that sticking to this gives us the best chance of highest probability for positive results."

The Cardinals also underwent a change in leadership on the player development side, a department now headed by Gary LaRocque, who was first hired as senior special assistant to Mozeliak in 2008 after a long career with the New York Mets and Los Angeles Dodgers.

"Under Gary I think you are seeing this system producing at a very high level," Mozeliak said. "He has been able to optimize how we do our business at the minor-league level. He has a very detailed curriculum for each player that does allow us to optimize their success."

The Cardinals, unlike many teams, actually own four of their seven minor-league franchises—the Triple A Memphis Redbirds, the Double A Springfield Cardinals, the high Class A Palm Beach Cardinals, and the rookie-level Gulf Coast League Cardinals. Only the low Class A Peoria Chiefs and rookie-level State College, Pennsylvania, Spikes and Johnson City, Tennessee, Cardinals have independent ownership.

"I don't think owning those franchises moves the needle all that much, but it does help," Mozeliak said. "The reason being, we in essence control the environment of what our players are in. If there is ever a breakdown or something isn't going as we would like, we can look at ourselves and make a change."

Another well-publicized ingredient to the organization's success has been the entire "Cardinal way" concept. Some people have characterized it as more of a moral standard, but it really is, Mozeliak said, just an organization-wide operating philosophy that emphasizes fundamentals and doing things the right way.

"A lot of people ask me what 'the Cardinal way' means," Mozeliak said. "I usually summarize it as, we understand and have great appreciation for our history, we understand what our job is today, but we also have an eye on our future. That's really what that means to me.

"When you are looking at a way to position your messaging, it just grew into 'the Cardinal way.' It's not something where we were trying to create our mission statement along those lines. We are really just trying to build our foundation from the bottom up of what we want our players to learn and understand.

"Not every team has that first part (our history). We inherited that. Look at the '20s, '30s, '40s—success. Fifties tough, '60s success, '70s tough, '80s success, '90s tough, and now currently success. What it shows you is a pretty good road map to capture a fan base."

Cardinals fans have indeed responded to the team's success. The team has drawn more than 3 million fans for each of the past 12 seasons and did not have a single crowd of less than 40,000 for any home game in the 2014 and 2015 seasons.

Mozeliak is smart enough, however, to realize that just because the Cardinals have achieved that success does not mean it is endowed to them in perpetuity. Other teams have noticed what they have done, and are quickly closing the gap.

"I think in general the league is catching up to us," he said. "I do still think we have a small advantage, but it's shrinking. It's the competitive nature of our business. Other people look at the best practices and try to copy and replicate. Our front office will continue to be challenged as we work hard for employee retention. We have a talented group and teams continue to look at us (to fill their) front office jobs."

Other teams no doubt envy the Cardinals' continuity at key positions in the organization. Since DeWitt bought the club 20 years ago, the team has had only two managers, Tony La Russa through 2011 and then Mike Matheny, and two general managers, Jocketty through 2007 and then Mozeliak. Most of the team's key scouting and player development personnel have worked in the organization for years.

"Not having to re-teach is important. You have people who understand what is expected," Mozeliak said. "For the most part I get a sense that people enjoy doing their jobs here."

One of the few positions which has been in flux over the years is scouting director, where Luhnow left to become GM of the Houston Astros, Dan Kantrovitz left to become assistant GM for the Oakland A's, and Chris Correa had to be let go after he was linked to an FBI investigation into a breach of the Astros' internal computer database.

Former Cardinals pitcher Randy Flores was hired by Mozeliak to serve as the new scouting director in August of 2015, another example of the organization looking for ways to take something it is doing well and try to do it even better.

"I don't think many people saw it coming, but I have a great appreciation for his business acumen and I think from a scouting standpoint he understands the game," Mozeliak said. "There will be an intense learning curve for him but I think from a leadership and management standpoint he will fit right in."

It was a decision, Mozeliak admits, designed to keep the Cardinals moving forward as an organization.

"I think what is most important to all of us who are part of that decision tree is that we understand this is a very fluid environment, a very competitive environment, and we need to adapt and change with it," he said.

"As the industry changes, as the competition changes, we have to stay in the forefront or on the cutting edge of innovation and understanding that collaboration with our group is important. Bill (DeWitt) and I both understand what today looks like, but we also have an eye on tomorrow."

That vision for the Cardinals of tomorrow is also the focus of all of the managers, coaches, roving instructors, and scouts whose job it is to identify and mold the players who will soon be wearing the Birds on the Bat, trying to continue to make the Cardinals baseball's best franchise.

2   MARK DeJOHN

BEING FIRED TURNED OUT TO BE ONE OF THE BEST THINGS THAT ever happened in Mark DeJohn's baseball life. It was the reason he got to spend 22 years with George Kissell.

"He was an amazing guy," DeJohn said. "He was a guy you just loved being around."

Kissell became a friend and mentor to DeJohn after the two met in 1986, when DeJohn was hired by the Cardinals as a minor-league manager. Years after Kissell's death his lessons are still being passed down to players through instructors and managers in the farm system such as DeJohn.

DeJohn has spent all but one of the last 30 years working for the Cardinals. One of the biggest reasons was the presence of Kissell.

"One of the things I tell guys all the time is that I wish they could have experienced George," DeJohn said. "Our managers would absolutely love him. The one thing you didn't want to do was get him mad. That's when he would go, 'Let me tell you something. I haven't told you everything I know.'"

What it didn't take long for DeJohn to learn after he came to work for the Cardinals was that Kissell knew a lot.

Originally drafted in the 23rd round by the Mets in 1971 as an infielder, DeJohn spent nine of his 13 years as a minor-league player at the Triple A level, both for the Mets and the Detroit Tigers. His playing career in the majors lasted for 24 games with the Tigers in 1982, in which he had four hits in 21 at-bats.

"I tell players now that, yeah, I played in the big leagues, but that wasn't my goal when I started," he said. "I got there because people liked me."

Once he started working for the Cardinals, it didn't take DeJohn long to realize that Kissell liked him, too.

The story of how DeJohn came to work for the Cardinals definitely includes a couple of odd twists and turns.

DeJohn might never have joined the Cardinals if things had worked out better for him when he was in his first season as a minor-league manager in 1985, having been hired by the Tigers following his playing career to manage their Double A team in Birmingham.

"They kind of made some promises to me and didn't fulfill them," DeJohn said. "They brought in somebody to watch us play a doubleheader in Orlando and it turned out it was Art Howe. They said if he wanted the job they were going to give it to him. I got mad and told the farm director to tell the general manager that I was mad and was going to look for a job in another organization at the end of the year.

"They called me the next morning and said, 'You can start looking now, you're fired.' It was a mistake on my part. I let my emotions take over instead of just calming down. It was almost like the Lord was leading me to the place where I needed to be. And Howe didn't take the job anyway."

It was May, a bad time to be looking for a coaching or managing job in the minor leagues.

"When I look back at it I can't tell you how devastated I was," DeJohn said. "It was a bad feeling driving home (to Connecticut). I couldn't find a job. We all think we're wanted by everybody. I was lucky to get back in."

After not knowing what his future held, DeJohn got a phone call from Art Stewart, the longtime scouting director of the Kansas City Royals. They had an opening for a coach at their short-season club in Eugene, Oregon, if DeJohn was interested. He immediately said yes.

What DeJohn didn't know then was how getting that job was going to lead him to Kissell and the Cardinals.

"The Royals' field coordinator was Howie Bedell," DeJohn said. "As far as I'm concerned he gave me the best advice I could possibly get. He asked me one day when we were sitting in the clubhouse in Eugene what my goals were. At that time I was younger, and I said I wanted to manage in the big leagues one day.

"He said, 'Well, how are you going to do that?' I said I didn't know. He said, 'Well, listen, what I would suggest you do is become the best baseball person you can possibly be—learn all facets of the game. And the way for you to do that is get with a good organization and stay there.'

"He named about four organizations, not mentioning the one he was with, and then he stopped and said, 'But if you really want to know baseball, get over there with George Kissell and the Cardinals.'"

DeJohn had spent time in the Instructional League with the Mets and Tigers and knew of Kissell.

"I always thought of him as a grumpy old man," DeJohn said. "Jim Riggleman helped me get the job and Lee Thomas hired me to manage in Savannah, Georgia, in 1986. Then I found out George was 66 years old. I thought, *He's ready to retire*. He wasn't even close. What I didn't know was the kind of energy he had."

DeJohn spent his first six years with the Cardinals managing in the minor leagues, moving from Savannah to Springfield to Johnson City to Louisville. After leaving the organization for one year, he returned, and after serving for six years as a coach on Tony La Russa's staff in the major leagues, went back to managing in the minors and spent time in New Haven, Tennessee, New Jersey, State College, and Batavia before becoming the field coordinator.

Kissell always floated through the organization, watching, listening, and offering advice when it was needed to both managers and players alike.

"He was like your father, like your grandfather, like your older brother," DeJohn said. "He was like that uncle you would love to see. He was just a special guy. He always treated me like I was his adopted son. It kind of bothered me in a sense but then I found out he was a hell of a dad. You just loved it when he came around."

Every time Kissell was around, DeJohn soon found out, a story usually followed.

"I'll never forget the time he came on the road with us that first year I was in Savannah," DeJohn said. "We were playing the Blue Jays in Florence, South Carolina, and we lost a tough game, in the ninth inning or something. I was mad, because you are real competitive when you are young.

"We were on the bus going back to the hotel and as we got closer George said, 'Hey Mark, when we get back to the hotel I'm going to get you a couple of aspirins. That was a real tough loss tonight.'"

As DeJohn remembers it, their conversation continued back and forth, with DeJohn insisting that he did not take aspirins and didn't want any aspirins and Kissell repeating that he was going to bring them to his room.

"I wasn't in my room five minutes and there was a knock on the door," DeJohn said. "I opened the door and George was standing there with two Bud Lights. He said, 'Here's a couple of aspirins. Take these and you'll feel better in the morning.'"

Another time Kissell was in town when the Cardinals wanted to look at a pitcher who had been released by another organization and arranged a tryout.

"I was standing off to the side of the pitcher watching him throw," DeJohn said. "George was at the other end, looking at the catcher. I was like, 'What is he doing?' When the tryout was over, George said, 'That guy's got a good arm.' I said, 'You were watching the catcher.' He said, 'I wasn't watching the catcher, Mark, I was listening for the ball. It had a little whistle to it. The guy's got a good arm.' I said, 'Well, son of a gun.' That was another side of George."

Kissell liked to have fun, on and off the field, as DeJohn learned a couple of years later, this time when he was managing in Johnson City, Tennessee.

"I had an old car, and George stuck a baseball behind the gas pedal," DeJohn said. "I couldn't start it because I couldn't push the pedal down. I didn't see the baseball. I finally slammed my foot down on the pedal and the ball shot out sideways and hit the door. I told one of the clubhouse kids to try to find out who had done it but nobody would own up to it. I finally found out it was George."

One of DeJohn's favorite stories about Kissell involves a trip a Korean team made to the Instructional League to work out with the Cardinals minor-leaguers, an Anheuser-Busch promotion.

"They had an interpreter with them, and he wrote everything down in a little black book—what George said, how we were doing things," DeJohn said. "George said, 'I'd like to get my hands on that guy's book.' When I asked him why, he said he wanted to see what he was writing down.

"I told him he was writing down all of the things he was saying and what we're doing. He said, 'I want to see it.' I said, 'George, if you saw it, how are you going to read it, it's all in Korean.' He said he wanted to see it anyway, but the guy never laid the book down. He always had it in his pocket.

"One day we went to Winter Haven to play the Indians, and the guy must have set the book down on the bench. Who do you think grabbed his book? George came over to me and said, 'Hey, Mark, I got his book. He put it down and I grabbed it.' So I asked him, 'What does it say?' And George said, 'I don't know. It's all in Korean.'

"The funniest part of the story was when the guy realized his book was missing. He was speaking in Korean, and even though we didn't understand him, you knew he was asking, 'Where's my book?' He was really kind of starting to get agitated. He looked at me and pointed his finger like he was threatening me. I told George he had better put the book back and he snuck it back when the guy wasn't looking. That was

George. We laughed like heck about it later. When he wanted to get something or do something, he found a way to get it done."

DeJohn also learned over their years together, however, that when it was time to be serious, nobody was more serious about baseball than Kissell. Operating with more independence than exists in the game today, Kissell would take a player's uniform away and order him to stay at the hotel for a couple of days if he found out the player was not hustling.

One time he was told a player had reported late to a game and Kissell instructed the manager to have him at second base after the game for "the tongue drill." Kissell proceeded to hit ground balls to the player, alternating between his right and left. Asked how long this was going to continue, Kissell replied, "Until his tongue is hanging out. That's why we call it the tongue drill."

It was Kissell, working as a special assistant on La Russa's staff in the majors in 2001, who hit ground balls every day to Fernando Vina even though he was in his seventies. Vina acknowledged that as the reason he won his first of two consecutive Gold Gloves that year.

"George didn't tell him how to catch a ground ball," DeJohn said. "George was the only one who hit grounders to him and he had a routine. He hit him the 12 or 14 different kinds of ground balls you can get in a game. He hit every one of them every day. It got Vina mentally prepared and his confidence level was up.

"When he won the Gold Glove, he had a replica made and sent it to George at his house as a way of saying thank you."

There is really no way to estimate how many players, managers, or coaches Kissell helped over the years, or an accurate way to measure what his presence, advice, and dedication meant to the success of the organization.

All DeJohn really knows is that Kissell's impact is still being felt today, from Jupiter, Florida, to Memphis and every place in between in the Cardinals system.

"A lot of what we still try to do, he started," DeJohn said. "The game has changed because there are different ways of teaching. We use video now, the Instructional League has changed, strength and conditioning have come into play. George would adapt to some of it. He would try to look at it as what is there to help the player. He would take something away from everything.

"He was a teacher. He always wanted to know why. Why were we doing something? If he was here today he would say the greatest word in the dictionary is *why*. Why did we do this? Why do we do that? He would just ask. He was just so full of knowledge and he never wanted to stop learning."

The Cardinals' operating manual is dedicated to Kissell. "A lot of the things in there are still things he came up with," DeJohn said.

Current players who never got to meet or learn from Kissell still walk by a framed photograph of a smiling Kissell at the Cardinals' complex in Jupiter. The clubhouse there bears his name, as does the "Kissell quad," a group of four fields on the far reaches of the complex.

Every year the Cardinals give out the "Kissell Award" to a staff member who has demonstrated excellence in player development. DeJohn has won the award twice, in 2003 and 2008.

"We talk about it a lot," DeJohn said. "There are people who have been in the game for 20 years and win the award and they are excited. It's a big thing. It's because of the name."

DeJohn knows his personality is different than Kissell's, but much of the way he tries to do his job stems from the way he was taught by Kissell, and his observations made over their time together.

One aspect of his job that DeJohn really enjoys, as did Kissell, is talking to the players. Two of the lessons he relays are about how quickly the game can humble you, and about how the name on the front of the jersey is more important than the name on the back.

Life in the minor leagues is different than the majors, DeJohn knows, because players are trying to win the game, but they also have to look out for themselves and their careers, with the goal of making it to the majors riding more on the results of their individual performances than whether the team won or lost a particular game.

The players do not operate in a vacuum, however, which is one of the lessons DeJohn tries to teach them as he, like Kissell did before him, travels to all of the Cardinals' minor-league affiliates.

"If a guy gets three hits in a game, he's going to be happy," DeJohn said. "But what if your team lost 10–1? That's one of the times you just have to be a professional when you go in the clubhouse. When you go home you should be happy; you did your job. But you have to respect the failure and the fact that the other people in the room are your teammates. George taught that to people.

"You have to know there is another day coming, and this game can humble you. That's just life. There is going to be a guy in the room who didn't do very well in the game. You have to learn to keep your mouth shut and just move on to the next day. The next day *you* could be that guy. There's a lot of lessons to learn in this game, and you do that by growing up and gaining experience.

"George taught people to put the organization before their personal agenda. You have to let your personal agenda take a backseat to what the organization needs. I think what you find out if you do that is that you will also achieve your goal.

"I also think players have to be realistic. Sometimes I think a player's self-evaluation actually can stand in their way. A player's opinion of himself doesn't really count. I tell players that if somebody tells them, 'You need to do this,' and then somebody else says it too, you'd better stop and think why people are saying or thinking that. That player needs to look himself in the mirror.

"We are all responsible for what we do. We have to be accountable. Everybody gets evaluated. What players sometimes don't realize is they might have gone 0-for-4, but they had two good at-bats. That's the process. Sometimes the process is more important than the results."

DeJohn makes his own schedule, which includes making at least two trips to see all seven teams in the Cardinals' minor-league system, including their team in the Dominican summer league, based at their academy. He usually spends at least five or six days with the team on every visit.

Especially at the lower levels, he is not looking for players who are ready for the major leagues. He is looking for indications of a player's ability.

"I see kids play a game and I will say to myself, 'If he can repeat that, he's a big-leaguer,'" DeJohn said. "A minor-leaguer does it on Monday, and then he doesn't do it again until Thursday.

Then he might not do it again until the following Monday. A big-leaguer does it every day. What I tell players is that they have got to take their best performance or what is close to their best performance and try to repeat it as many times as they can.

"If you are only doing that once a week, try to get to where by the end of the season, you are doing it three times a week. We are looking for marked improvement. We want to see if guys playing at Peoria are going to be good enough to play at Palm Beach next year."

Of all the things DeJohn picked up from Kissell in their two decades together, one stands out above the rest.

"The biggest thing I took from him was his love of the Cardinals," DeJohn said. "There isn't a guy who loved the Cardinals more than George Kissell. When you are around people like that, you learn what the organization is all about, the people that we have here.

"A lot of people talk about 'the Cardinal way,' but what that really means to me is the closeness we have as a group. We all get along, and we are all pulling in the right direction."

DeJohn knows there are differences between the way the Cardinals run their farm system and the way other teams operate, and he is not afraid to say that the people working for the Cardinals do not have an exclusive monopoly on answers.

"When we sit in meetings we certainly don't think that we are smarter than anybody else," DeJohn said. "What we try to do is get along—that starts from the top and goes all the way down. When there are problems we get them solved. We've got good people here and they know what they are doing."

DeJohn tells the story about a conversation he had while visiting the rookie team in Johnson City, where Chris Swauger was in his first year as a manager in 2015 after many years playing in the system. A player was getting a new pair of shoes from his agent, and they included some neon colors. The player wanted to know if he would be allowed to wear those shoes.

The answer was no.

"I told Chris later, you don't need to ask," DeJohn said. "Just ask yourself, 'Would you wear those shoes as a Cardinal?' He said no. I said, 'If you ask yourself the question and you know the answer, you don't need to ask me. You can solve the situation.'

"The important point is that as a rookie-league manager, what you allow is going to go on to the next level. A player is going to continue to do the same thing. And if another manager tells him no, you know the first thing out of the player's mouth is going to be, 'Swauger let me do it.'"

Evaluating players involves a lot more than just measuring a player's ability. One of the qualities DeJohn values most in a player is desire.

"We've all seen a lot of talented guys who didn't have the desire needed for them to be a big-leaguer," DeJohn said. "You really have to want it to be a big-league player regardless of your talent. The example we use now is Yadier Molina. Nobody has his desire. It's amazing. If you can find a player who does have the talent and you can match that with desire, now you have something."

One of the lessons DeJohn tries to pass along to players, especially those just coming into the organization, is to get the most out of the experience while they are there.

"When we have the 30 or so new guys in the room, I tell them their goal is to play in the major leagues, but that is a very tough thing to do," DeJohn said. "You have an opportunity, try to take advantage of it. But there is no shame if you fail to reach that goal as long as you put everything you had into it. This might just be a steppingstone to something else. It's all part of a big plan."

DeJohn, like Kissell before him, also looks to the players in the organization to see who he thinks can move into another capacity when their playing days are over. He did that with Swauger, and there are others he thinks will make that transition in the years to come.

It's all part of Kissell's Cardinal way.

"That's what George did with people," DeJohn said. "It's how you keep the continuity of what we are doing, because they already know the system, they understand how it works. And they know what is expected."

So even though Swauger joined the organization as a first-year player the same year Kissell died, he is still getting the same benefits and knowledge, passed down from instructors such as DeJohn.

"In order for you to achieve your goals in the game, there are going to be many people who come across your path who will help you along the way. But there's going to be only a few special people, and George was one of them to me," DeJohn said. "I'm lucky. I left one time and it was a mistake on my part. George got me back.

"His knowledge was unbelievable, but it was his love of the Cardinals that rubs off on you. You can't help it. I've been to his house in St. Petersburg and it was all Cardinals stuff. I'm surprised it wasn't painted red on the outside. He was a beautiful man.

"It's almost like George is watching out for you. You just saw his love of the organization on a daily basis. To be a part of something that he loved so much, it's like being a Cardinal is something special. It certainly was to George."

And it is to others, too.

3   MIKE SHILDT

THE SMALL BLACK BOOK IS ONE OF MIKE SHILDT'S MOST PRIZED
possessions.

He takes it with him almost everywhere and reads it daily.
He goes to it when he has a question, or when he is looking for
guidance on a troubling issue.

It's his physical connection to the wisdom and teachings of
George Kissell, and as a manager in the Cardinals' farm system
since 2009, Shildt has observed firsthand how Kissell's ideas
and suggestions have more than stood the test of time.

The book is an exact replica of the one Kissell kept himself
as his manual for much of his career with the Cardinals. It was
a gift from Kissell's son, Dr. Richard Kissell, who is the team
physician for the Double A Springfield Cardinals. Shildt was
given a copy after the 2012 season, Shildt's first as that team's
manager. Others in the organization received a copy as well.

"I almost couldn't verbalize the sentiment," Shildt said of his
reaction to getting the book. "First of all, that he put that together and then the thoughtfulness to give it to me and others.
Beyond that is just the book itself. When you read it you can

feel the passion, the attention to detail. You appreciate the years and the wisdom that goes into it.

"It means a lot for a lot of reasons and it's a blessing to be able to have it. Dr. Kissell was nice enough to put in a couple of pages to take notes. George always wanted you to improve on things, and Dr. Kissell told me, 'George would want you to make some notes in it. That would please him.' I just can't do it. I take notes every day, but I just can't write them in that book. I don't feel that it is appropriate or that I'm worthy."

Shildt knew all about the book from his years in the organization and the time he did get to spend with Kissell before Kissell's death in 2008. (Shildt's father passed away on the same date, October 7, as Kissell, though in a different year.)

Shildt thinks of Kissell every time he picks up the book.

"I look at it, I meditate on it," Shildt said. "It helps when things maybe go a little sideways. It's a good place for solace. It's almost like a Bible, really. I share it with people, some of the newer staff members and players."

One of Shildt's go-to sections of the book is for managers, starting with two questions: do you have a checklist, and are you an organization man?

"It makes you think. Are you going about things in the right way?" Shildt said. "We are fundamentally based in this organization but sometimes you can get away from it or lose focus. I go back through my checklist. There are questions I ask myself most days."

Kissell's lingering influence in the Cardinals organization is felt beyond the pages of the little black book. Shildt didn't get the chance to spend as much time with Kissell as he would have liked, but was around him enough to understand how skilled he was and how important his knowledge of the game, and of people, has been to the organization's continuing success.

"His influence is everywhere," Shildt said. "I don't want to pontificate that I spent a lot of time with George but I was fortunately blessed to get to know him near the end of his life. On a day-to-day basis I am more of a second-generation descendent. But you talk about a wake of influence—it's only growing, which is the impressive thing about it. George is the patriarch.

"I grew up in the (Baltimore) Orioles organization and for 25 years they were the winningest organization in baseball. But they lost their way because they lost the people associated with it. George was able to identify people who value what we do here and he would pour into them. We have people who are willing to respect that mindset and tradition."

Shildt got another reminder of that during spring training in 2008. He was still relatively new to the organization, having originally been hired as a scout before gradually switching over to working on the field in uniform. He had never even been to spring training with the Cardinals when he was asked to run the camp in 2008.

In addition to Kissell, one of the people he talked to about the assignment was Pop Warner, another Kissell disciple who had been in the organization since 1991 as a player, coach, and manager.

"Right before camp started I went up to Pop and said, 'I want to put a theme on camp,'" Shildt said. "He looked at me like, 'What's wrong with you? What do you mean?' He said, 'We don't need a theme. We're the Cardinals.'

"What I realized he meant was that we don't need to search for an identity. We're about doing the little things, doing them well;

executing the fundamentals, playing the game smart, and playing it in a highly competitive manner. It was stuff I already knew,
but the point being there was an accountability there. When you
start to get off the page a little bit, somebody is going to tell you
where the page is. You have that anchor to draw from."

Shildt had to perhaps rely more on Kissell's suggestions in
2015 than he had in previous years because of his new assignment
to manage the Cardinals' Triple A team in Memphis. He was
working with players at a different point in their careers, many of
whom were either on the verge of making it to the major leagues,
such as outfielder Stephen Piscotty, or on the way back from
playing in the majors.

One of the challenges Shildt has been able to overcome in his
career with the Cardinals is the fact that he never played professional baseball, even though he—literally—grew up around
the game and knew from an early age he wanted to have a career in baseball.

Shildt grew up in Charlotte, North Carolina, and was about
eight years old when his mother got a job working in the office
for the Orioles' Double A affiliate. Baseball was already in the
Shildt family blood: his father had proposed to his mother during an Orioles game at Memorial Stadium.

"I started basically when she started," Shildt said. "I got $5
a game to chase down foul balls. I stood outside behind home
plate and waited for balls to come outside the stadium. I chased
them down and returned them. That was how I earned my pay."

Shildt quickly moved inside the stadium, where he worked
as one of the clubhouse boys, and where his baseball education
really began. It was 1980, and the team's star was a 19-year-old
shortstop named Cal Ripken Jr.

"I shined Cal's shoes every day," Shildt said. "I made a lot of observations about how guys carried themselves and Cal was a great example of that. I watched how he worked."

The impact Ripken had on an impressionable youngster is one of the reasons Shildt wears uniform No. 8, Ripken's number during his career with the Orioles, even though he wore number 12 that year in Charlotte, Shildt said.

Even at that young age, Shildt was watching and learning. When the games began, he went up to the press box, where for several years his job was to run the scoreboard.

"I was smarter than I was talented, even though there is not a high bar there," Shildt said. "I loved the game and I studied the game. I wasn't really trying to learn anything specific then but I was around some amazing baseball people.

"I think what helped me as much as anything was running the scoreboard, which I did for four or five years. Guys were always gracious to me. I grew up as a clubhouse guy, so I can relate to our clubhouse guys now, and I hung out with the reporters in the press box and I learned about their side of the business."

Mostly, however, Shildt just watched the game. He had to be aware of every pitch to correctly display it on the scoreboard.

"Somehow if you watch anything enough you learn something," Shildt said. "I got an education in baseball at a really young age."

Shildt was also playing the game and after high school walked on to the team at North Carolina–Asheville. He was a freshman there when he learned he was legally blind in his left eye.

"I went through the eye exam and I thought (the doctor) was messing with me," Shildt said. "I told him, 'I realize I probably don't see 20-20,' and he said, 'You probably don't see 20-400.'"

More exams revealed that Shildt actually suffered from keratoconus, a degenerative disease, in both eyes. He was able to correct his vision with contact lenses for a while but eventually had to receive cornea transplants or risk going blind.

"I had no clue," Shildt said about his vision problems. "I drove a car. I didn't know what I wasn't able to see. I just compensated."

While in college, Shildt had a part-time job working as a bellman at the Radison Hotel in Asheville. One day he saw Willie Stargell come in the door. Stargell was a roving instructor for the Atlanta Braves, and they were in town to play against Asheville.

When he was 11, Shildt had seen Stargell from a different vantage point. His mother, because of her job with the Charlotte O's, had gotten a ticket for Game 7 of the World Series between the Orioles and Pittsburgh Pirates. Shildt, naturally an Orioles fan, had flown to Baltimore, stayed at his aunt's house, and went to the game, hoping to see the Orioles celebrate a world championship. Instead the Pirates won 4–1, in part thanks to a two-run home run by Stargell.

That memory had stayed with Shildt, who went into the hotel kitchen and made up a fruit basket, which he took up to Stargell's room.

"I told him it was compliments of the hotel, but I also said, 'I want you to know I was a big Orioles fan and was 11 years old and was in the stands for Game 7 of the 1979 World Series and you broke my heart when you hit that home run off (Scott) McGregor,'" Shildt said. "He looked at me and said, 'You didn't poison my grapes, did you?'"

Another vivid memory Shildt has from his college days came after getting an at-bat in a game at Tennessee. He was on the bus back to Asheville when he said to a buddy that he just re-alized his future, if it was in baseball, was not going to be as a player. He already possessed enough knowledge of the game to self-evaluate his own talent level.

Shildt was able to work as an assistant with the college team for a couple of years after earning his degree in business, when an opening came up to coach at an inner-city high school in Charlotte a day before the season began.

"The school historically had not been very good in baseball but had been super strong in football and basketball," Shildt said. "We took a beating that first year. The next year we had 11 players on the varsity team and started a JV program with nine. Nobody could be sick or miss school because then we couldn't play. The varsity team went 12–9."

Shildt's real education that year, however, came inside the walls of West Charlotte High School. He had arrived for the start of the school year expecting to be a full-time substitute teacher but instead was told the school had a class for him.

"They literally took me down the hall and shoved me in a room," Shildt said. "I found out it was a cross-category class for kids with emotional or behavioral disabilities or kids with physical handicaps. It was quite an experience, rewarding and trying. It was an opportunity for me to start developing my own experiences in leadership.

"It made no sense to me how they operated that class. State law said you could have up to 12 kids in the class and we had 14. Half were on probation for bringing a gun or knife to school. Then we had learning-disability students who were sweet but couldn't add two plus two. They were some really scared kids who had not been given a lot of love.

"We would have people come in to observe who were qualified to teach the class and they would excuse themselves to go to the restroom and never come back. The school discouraged me from mainstreaming with the rest of the student body."

Shildt really didn't know what he was doing except trying to maintain order, but at the end of the year the principal told him he had done the best job of anybody they had ever had teaching that class.

"I challenged him back and said, 'I didn't do anything for these kids.' He said he wanted me back and I told him to find somebody who was qualified to teach those kids," Shildt said. "He said, 'Well, you helped them,' and I asked, 'What's your definition of help?' He said, 'We had no mainstream incidents.' I said that shouldn't be the bar for those kids."

That experience did help Shildt realize, however, that he might be able to help young people, and that perhaps the best place he could do that was on a baseball field.

"I think my spiritual gift might be to understand how to help people," he said. "Baseball has given me that opportunity. Those kids were no different than other kids; they just were battling different circumstances."

Shildt remained as the school's baseball coach for another year, and that season the team reached the city's championship game before losing 3–1 to one of the best teams in the state.

"I still keep in touch with a lot of those kids," Shildt said. "That group let me cut my teeth and learn how to coach."

Shildt's next coaching opportunity came as an assistant at North Carolina–Charlotte. "The opportunity was about experience and not a whole lot about compensation," he said.

Wanting to stay close to home after his father's death, Shildt decided to use his business degree and opened a youth base-ball training academy. He raised money to help cover the costs for players and teams which could not afford it, and with the business doing well, he decided it was time to look for another challenge.

Shildt had become friends with Gary Randall, who worked for the Major League Scouting Bureau, and Randall helped him land a spot in Scout School in 2002.

"Candidly I didn't really ever want to scout," Shildt said. "But I told Gary I didn't think I was growing. I told him I would like to try to find something. I don't know if he told anybody or not, but one day in December of 2003 I got a phone call out of the blue from John Mozeliak."

Mozeliak said the Cardinals had an opening for a scout in the Carolinas and Virginia and wanted to know if Shildt was inter-ested. The two talked for 90 minutes and Mozeliak promised to get back to Shildt within a couple of days.

It was the week before Christmas, and Shildt was a little discouraged when he didn't hear from Mozeliak. Finally on the afternoon of Christmas Eve, Mozeliak called and said the Cardinals wanted to hire him and arranged for him to fly to St. Louis in January.

By that time, Shildt had decided to take the job—if the Cardinals also gave him a chance to coach. While he was in the team's offices, he was left alone for a few minutes and casually walked into the office of Bruce Manno, the director of player development at the time.

"I told him I was taking a scouting job but part of the deal was that I was going to get to coach and that Mo was going to talk to him about it," Shildt said. "He was like, 'Who are you again?'"

Shildt got his wish, and after the amateur draft was over in 2004, he went to the Cardinals' short-season team in New Jersey as a coach.

"That's where my whole world opened up," Shildt said. "Whatever I thought I knew was a morsel to what I've learned from Mark DeJohn."

Shildt served as a coach for DeJohn for the next three years while taking on more and more responsibility—coaching third, then serving as the manager for some games. Shildt was so excited he actually got ejected from two games in about a 10-day span.

"DeJohn was like, 'Dude, you've got to calm down,'" Shildt said. "He let me act like I was the manager, but he was standing right beside me and kept asking me questions: 'Why are you doing this? What are you doing that for?' It was like he was 15 steps ahead of me. My head was spinning.

"I had no clue he was grooming me to be a manager. I never thought there was a chance I was going to manage. I thought in the best-case scenario I was going to be a hitting coach in rookie ball for the rest of my life, and I was fine with that.

"The one thing I was smart enough to do when I got in this organization was just listen and not talk. The only time I spoke was to ask a question or clarify something."

DeJohn's influence helped Shildt get the chance to run the Instructional League program for a brief period, and then came the chance to run spring training in 2008.

"I had been to one spring training game in my life, between Toronto and Philadelphia, in 1991 in Clearwater when I was on spring break," Shildt said. "Luckily I had a lot of help from a lot of other people, managers, and instructors."

DeJohn had specifically asked that Shildt be his coach in

2006, and by 2008, after serving as a coach in Johnson City, the Cardinals thought he was ready to be a manager. He took over the rookie league team the next season, one of the few people to actually get that opportunity without ever having played in professional baseball at any level.

"People threw jabs at it occasionally but I don't give it a second thought anymore," Shildt said. "I used to worry it was going to hold me back. I had to earn my way. I feel to some degree I've put my time in. I did a lot of stuff outside of pro ball. I slept on some couches. I coached a lot of Legion ball. I sold a lot of ads for programs so I could eat. I put my time in.

"I took every opportunity to coach as much as they would let me. I gained experience traded out for compensation and comfort. I developed a personal mantra that I was comfortable with what I didn't know but confident in what I did know. That served me well.

"I knew I had a baseline of being able to think the game and I knew I was going to work hard and be organized and more importantly cared about the greater good of the players and the organization. That's why I think I've been able to fit in."

One of the first realities that Shildt came to know and appreciate about the organization was how many employees had been there for decades, many of whom had never worked anywhere else.

"The common trait among those people was that they cared more about the Birds on the Bat than they did about themselves," Shildt said. "That's a special, unique place. It felt like home to me for that reason. I wanted to help young people and I wanted to be with an organization that does things right and is serious about excellence."

Shildt was 40 years old when he got the chance to manage Johnson City, and led the team to a winning season, going 37–30. His own personal growth, however, was not completely measured by those won-loss numbers.

One of the first things he learned, another lesson passed down from Kissell, was that players won't care about how much you know until they know how much you care.

Working with players who in some cases were playing as professionals or living on their own for the first time meant a lot of Shildt's time was spent dealing with off-the-field concerns as well as teaching baseball fundamentals.

Instead of having those players live in hotels or apartments, the organization tried to arrange for each player to live with a host family.

"Some kids are able to handle freedoms, but the host family situation typically worked pretty well," Shildt said. "It helped them with their diet because they were fed better and had a little bit of accountability for what they were doing."

Shildt learned quickly at Johnson City that comfort was a key ingredient to a player's success at that level.

"A lot of players are inconsistent at the lower levels and it's harder for Latino players based on their age, another culture, and different factors such as playing under the lights maybe for the first time," he said. "Their level of consistency is harder to replicate.

"Getting them to be comfortable with everything as quickly as possible is important. There are more obstacles for Latino players. We just tried to make everything as comfortable and consistent as possible so they could just go out and perform."

The players—for the most part different players—did that in

Shildt's next two years in Johnson City, winning Appalachian League championships in 2010 and 2011.

That provided another valuable lesson for those players, Shildt believes.

"Development supersedes winning and is the primary responsibility of the minor-league department, to develop championship-caliber players, but within that I do believe teaching guys how to win is invaluable," Shildt said. "At the end of the day, when they get to the big leagues, they are playing to win. To know how that looks and the dedication and focus that it takes on a daily basis—that's what we strive for.

"To me, the most beneficial part of being able to play in minor-league playoffs is the opportunity and evaluation you get for the players—to see how they respond to that atmosphere, how they deal with it and react to it. I have seen lots of examples of guys growing from those opportunities. Our pitching coach, Bryan Eversgerd, has a good quote which we use a lot: 'Who you are is what you do when you are at your most uncomfortable.' We want to see where guys are when they are a little uncomfortable. When you are in a playoff or championship scenario, how are they going to learn from that? Hopefully what they learn during the year is not to do anything different when it becomes a 'pressure' situation. You're either applying pressure or feeling it, and you always want to apply it."

After three years in Johnson City, Shildt was promoted all the way to Double A Springfield for the 2012 season—and promptly led his team to the Texas League title, his third championship in as many years.

Shildt is quick to point out, however, that any minor-league championship is an "organization" championship, citing the variables of the health of teams above you and the involvement of the rovers and other personnel who work with the players during the year.

"I was fortunate to be there because it was such a rewarding year because of the opportunities to see guys grow," he said. "There was pain involved with that. Word it any way you want—through growth comes pain or through pain comes growth. What I respected and appreciated about that group was pretty much at every step, at every turn, those players on that team who got met with individual or collective adversity continued to push, continued to grow, continued to learn. They continued to understand what it was about. It was a hungry group that wanted to do well."

Shildt's success in his first six seasons as a manager led the Cardinals to promote him again for the 2015 season, to the Triple A Memphis Redbirds.

Triple A is generally considered the hardest level to manage in the minors, and Shildt knew he was taking on a challenging position, realizing a higher emphasis needed to be placed on dealing with the players' emotions and mental focus more than actual baseball instruction.

"What I realized here is the biggest service I can have is to just be consistent in how I deal with guys and give them the respect they have earned at this level," Shildt said. "The biggest thing I have learned is how to empathize with this group of guys. We have guys who are so close to their dream, or coming back from their dream, and they are having to deal with all the different distractions and expectations of the organization. I just try to do the best I can to teach the game but also to help guys understand how to deal with things.

"The reality is what can help you the most is how to emotionally deal with so many different things. It's a teaching challenge and a growth process. There are days I miss the physical baseball instruction, the first and thirds, the cutoffs and relays—all that stuff. But like George would say, it's just trying to give people as many tools in the toolbox as possible. This is just another tool for me to help them develop as a player.

"People say Triple A is the hardest place in general to manage, play, whatever. I have to try to do the best I can to teach the game but also to help guys understand how to deal with things. You have to teach things differently at this level."

Trying to make certain players are ready for the major leagues when the opportunity comes up also is a different responsibility.

"I'm a messenger for Mike (Matheny), Mo (John Mozeliak), and the big-league staff and for Gary (LaRocque)," Shildt said. "The message to me is to understand what they want. What are their expectations? And then it's my responsibility to make sure everybody in the clubhouse understands what those expectations are—the kind of player they want you to be, what you need to be ready to contribute. I have to understand what the player needs to do to be able to meet those expectations. Sometimes it can be a bit overwhelming, which is why we are very process driven."

Because of injuries, the major-league Cardinals had to dip down to Memphis for multiple reinforcements during the 2015 season, and Shildt was proud of how those players went up and met or exceeded the expectations of the organization when called upon. What Shildt was happy to see was how their Memphis teammates cheered the success of the players promoted to St. Louis, something he wasn't positive would be the case.

"When Stephen Piscotty hit his first homer in St. Louis, everybody was watching and cheering," Shildt said. "When Greg Garcia got a big hit, everybody was excited. Guys who have been other places tell me that's not a very normal thing. It's another example of how the Cardinals get people to care more about the greater good than about themselves."

Some of the players promoted to the majors later had to come back to Memphis, which presented Shildt with another challenge.

"They do a good job in St. Louis of explaining to guys what's going on and what they need to work on. When they come back, they come back with a sense of purpose," Shildt said. "Knowing that they need to work on a certain pitch or whatever it is helps them focus. Having that sense of purpose is important.

"It does take a while to get them going again and let them get their head around being here again. Memphis is a great place. It's a great setup and a great park with a great staff. But even with all of those great things, it's not St. Louis. As good as it is, it's not close. It's just different. I empathize with these guys because of that."

Shildt also helps players identify the areas they need to work on by having everybody on the team complete a progress report midway through the season. It is something which is done at every level of the organization.

"We get them to fill it out, listing what they think are their strengths, areas that need improvement, and then come up with a plan," Shildt said. "What's important is for me to find out what the player knows, to establish that baseline. After the player fills it out, the coaches go over it and then we set up a half-hour meeting with each player.

"We ask them for their thoughts. We learn so much from that. It gives them ownership, because they are telling you where they think they are, and then you can give them your thoughts so everybody can get on the same page. It is just another way of opening up communication.

"We want them invested in the plan, so they can continue to grow. Invariably they get it, and then they take off and rise to whatever level of ability they have. That's all you are asking for."

For many players, their ability—combined with their work ethic and desire—will result in Shildt getting a phone call from Mozeliak with the news that a particular player is being promoted to the big leagues.

It is then Shildt's assignment to inform the player of the news.

"It's by far the best part of my job," he said. "Telling people they are going to the big leagues for the first time is so special. To be able to share a moment like that with somebody, it doesn't matter what kind of day you are having or how you are playing. It's just unbelievable."

During the 2015 season, Shildt got to break that news to Piscotty, Mitch Harris, Ed Easley, Cody Stanley, Tim Cooney, and Marcus Hatley, just as he had done in previous seasons when Trevor Rosenthal, Carlos Martinez, and Marco Gonzales made the jump directly from Double A.

"What I appreciate the most is that the general public really has no clue what these guys go through and the dedication, the sacrifice, and the mental and physical toughness that it takes to work your way through a system and become a big-league player," Shildt said. "When you start out there are no guarantees that the end result is going to be what you want.

"When you are able to tell a guy that he's being rewarded for all that sacrifice, hard work, and dedication—going back to when they first started playing baseball as a young child—all the things they did to play this game and chase their dreams and go for it. To get the payoff is unbelievable."

Recalling all of those moments, and how special each one was, is a feeling Shildt never wants to forget.

"You try to paint the picture of players at the lower levels about what kind of player you need to be to get to the big leagues," he said. "Some of them have an understanding that it is out there but it seems a long way away. Some guys will never get there and never get to fulfill their potential.

"Our job is to help them realize their potential and give them the tools they need to get there. That is our job. That's why we are here. That's the definition of player development. That's why we have our jobs."

4 MITCH HARRIS

UNTIL HE ARRIVED IN JUPITER, FLORIDA, FOR THE START OF SPRING training in February of 2015, the Mitch Harris story was always about the journey—the unusual path he traveled for seven years, and the long odds and obstacles he had faced in pursuit of his dream of playing major-league baseball.

Something changed when Harris walked into the Cardinals clubhouse, however. That journey, which had taken Harris around the world, was no longer what was most important to him.

Some of the people in the room knew the story from having played with Harris at minor-league stops the previous two years. Others he was meeting for the first time didn't know why the right-handed pitcher was unique among the non-roster players in the room, all of whom had their own story to tell.

"I think they have an idea," Harris said of his teammates, "but I don't know to what extent or where we started. To me, if they know, that's cool; if they don't, I don't care.

"To me, the first thing is I want to be a good teammate and a good player. After that, if they figure out the story, that's cool. I don't want that to be the center of attention or the first thing that comes to mind when you hear the name 'Mitch Harris.' I want people to think, *He's a great teammate, and a guy we want to pitch in tough situations*. After that, they can say, 'Oh yeah, that's a really cool story.'"

Harris' story, and his journey, really began in 2004. When he was a senior at South Point High School in Belmont, North Carolina, he was weighing the decision about where to go to college. One scholarship offer he considered was from Lee University in Cleveland, Tennessee, where his father was an alumnus. It was also near his grandparents' home and had a quality baseball program.

Another school he was considering was the U.S. Naval Academy.

"We started talking about all of the different venues and I told him that's a decision for you and the Lord," said Cy Harris, Mitch's father. "You all make the decision and let me know. He came back and said, 'I think I want to go to the Naval Academy.'"

While baseball was a factor, Harris also was thinking about the education he would receive at the Academy, where he wanted to major in engineering.

He also knew he was making a serious commitment—once a cadet begins his junior year, he is obligated to serve five years of active duty in the Navy following graduation. At that time, having gone undrafted in baseball out of high school, Harris did not know if he had a future in baseball, but he knew he had one in the Navy.

It was when Harris was a junior at the Academy that the baseball world began to pay attention to the impressive numbers he was putting up in the Patriot League. Paul Kostacopoulos had already noticed Harris' talent, immediately after he was hired as Navy's coach.

"I didn't know anyone's name, and we had maybe 60 guys running around the field," Kostacopoulos said. "Mitch started to throw, and after the third pitch I knew this kid was special. He had size and he had an electric arm. The first pitch was 89, then 91, then 92. I said, 'OK, we got ourselves a guy.'"

Scouts who descended on the Academy in Annapolis, Maryland, could project Harris' ability as a baseball prospect, but they were unfamiliar with the Navy's rules. Some teams asked Harris if there was a way they could buy out his Navy commitment so he could begin a pro career immediately, as could juniors at almost any other college in the country.

"We couldn't give them a straight answer because we didn't have a straight answer," Harris said. "The Navy never gave us a true answer."

There was another issue as well.

"There is a clause in the contract that says if they believe you are trying to get out of a commitment, they can make you serve enlisted and take your commission away," Harris said. "I didn't want to flirt with that."

Harris discussed the situation with his father.

"I told him it was his choice, but that baseball was a business," Cy Harris said. "If you hurt yourself, they are going to throw you to the curb. You won't have a degree and you won't be able to play baseball because you're hurt. If you stay and get your degree, you can get a job anywhere."

Harris told teams he was not going to sign until after graduation. The Braves drafted him in the 24th round anyway. Harris stayed. Most of the scouts left. Many didn't return the following year because Harris was unable to pitch for the first six weeks of his senior season. He had hit a home run on the final at-bat of fall ball, but tripped as he rounded third base while high-fiving a teammate, falling on his right shoulder.

"It went from a funny moment to being not funny a moment later," Harris said.

The Cardinals were still intrigued, however, and decided to take a chance on Harris in the 13th round of the 2008 draft. They gave him a $10,000 signing bonus and wished him Godspeed during his Navy career. Maybe they would see him in five years, perhaps sooner, perhaps never.

There were a couple of points during his Navy service when Harris thought he was close to an early exit from his active duty assignment, in exchange for more time in the Reserves. Each time his request ultimately was denied.

"He knew the deal," Kostacopoulos said. "He was not surprised by that. Mitch has this way about him that I think came from his parents and family, that no matter what adversity comes his way, no matter what bend in the road or disappointment he has, he truly is able to handle it.

"He does something that I think a lot of young people can learn from—he takes his disappointments and turns them into determination. Rather than letting the disappointments define who he is, he spins that around. I think it fuels him to be determined to do what he wants to do. He's always been like that."

It took almost the entire five years—four years and eight months, to be exact—before Harris was allowed to leave. Unable to do anything other than play catch occasionally during his time away, much of which was spent on three overseas deployments, not even Harris knew what to expect.

"My body was going to tell me. I said I was going to give myself a couple of years to get back into form and get back in the swing of things," Harris said. "If it wasn't progressing I would move on. Obviously things progressed probably a little quicker than anyone imagined."

When he first put on a Cardinals uniform, Harris was not able to throw his fastball much harder than 80 miles per hour. His command, naturally, was another issue, and he needed work on his secondary pitches as well.

"I think they got a 27-year-old boy with a 22-year-old arm," Cy Harris said. "It had been dormant, but it also had little to no wear and tear."

Because of the long layoff, the Cardinals did not expect immediate results. They were willing to be patient with Harris, as long as they saw progress, but because of his age—playing in a short-season rookie league in State College, Pennsylvania—Harris knew time was not on his side.

He achieved a lot of notoriety, however, because of the almost unprecedented nature of what he was trying to do.

As proud as he was of serving his country, Harris confessed to his father that he was tired of all the attention given to his background.

"He told me, 'I'm sick of this being the story,'" Cy Harris said. "I said, 'Let your arm be the story.' When he was little one time we were going somewhere to play and a guy was throwing pretty hard and he said, 'Dad, I can hit that guy.' I said, 'Tell me with your stick.' It's the same thing with his arm.

"That other stuff will fade. I told him that other stuff will always be there because that's your history. But your arm should do the talking."

Two years after manager Mike Matheny put Harris into a spring training game against the Mets—as a way to honor him, not knowing the future—Harris was back on the mound at Roger Dean Stadium in March of 2015. After giving up two homers and retiring only one hitter in that game in 2013, Harris was now throwing fastballs at close to 95 miles per hour, breaking off cutters, and showing a quality split-finger pitch.

Adam Wainwright was in the dugout 24 months earlier when Harris took the mound. He was there in 2015, too.

"His fastball just wasn't there," Wainwright said of Harris' first appearance. "His command wasn't there. I was thinking, *What in the world is this guy doing in big league camp?* They said 'He's been in the Navy, fighting overseas,' and I went, 'Nevermind.'"

True to his goal, Harris was no longer being called on to pitch as a ceremonial gesture, but to find out if he was ready to be a major-leaguer.

"He's worked hard and I just respect so much what he did (for the country)," Wainwright said. "When I saw him pitch I said, 'This guy's got a chance.' Before it was a good story about how he came back to play baseball. It was heartwarming. Now it's like, 'OK, I can see this.' This guy has got a big-league arm."

That's all Harris wanted to hear.

Sitting in a seat just to the right of home plate, Cy Harris admitted to a little bit of anxiety as his son came in a game to pitch against the Miami Marlins. He had experienced the feeling before.

Harris, who spent 28 years as a minister of music and is now the pastor of pastoral care and facilities at North Cleveland Church of God in Cleveland, Tennessee, was in the stands when Harris made the opening day start for the Bourne Braves in the prestigious Cape Cod League in the summer of 2007, after his junior year at Navy.

"He was like a little fish in a big pond," Cy Harris said. "They announced the players for the other team. I don't remember who they were, but they were All-America guys. One guy was a batting champion. Another guy walked to the plate and had tree trunks for legs."

Harris allowed just three hits and one run in six innings en route to the victory that day.

"I've always tried to be unbiased," Harris said. "After that game I knew there was a good chance."

Watching his son take on major-league hitters, even in spring training, was a new experience for Harris. He watched his son allow a single and a walk, before getting a double-play grounder to end the inning. Harris followed with a 1-2-3 inning after returning to the mound.

His dad, who pulled out a video camera for the first two batters so he could send the tape back home to his wife, who could not take off work to accompany him to Florida, was able to exhale as his son's work day ended.

"We have always talked about when something's not right, take your time and get your composure," Cy Harris said. "He walked around the mound and did that. It's like when we play golf and he's hooking the ball. Why? It's about adapting and making adjustments. It was exciting that he got out of it."

During his short visit to Jupiter, Cy Harris also watched as his son signed countless autographs and heard stadium workers offer unsolicited praise about his son's makeup and character.

"This was his lifelong dream," Harris said. "A lot of sweat and tears and heartache have gone into this. I'm proud for him;

he set the goal and accomplished it. He's my son. I stood up there and watched little kids come up and he probably signed as many or more autographs than anybody. That used to be him. I know what it meant to him when he was a kid. It's the little things that make a difference. He sees that too. I told him, 'Don't lose that.'"

Kostacopoulos, for one, does not see that happening.

"What he is doing is a great story, but honestly it's more about who we graduate here (at Navy) than Mitch being a professional athlete," Kostacopoulos said. "It puts a spotlight on the fact we have special young men and women here who have amazing talents, all kinds of different talents. Ultimately they've chosen to serve our country.

"Mitch understands that our military makes unbelievable sacrifices so we can do what we do. He gets that. We have professional baseball; we have a free country. That's engrained in him."

That, too, is part of Harris' story.

"We overuse words and hyperbole in our society now, but this is an amazing story of many, many triumphs, probably many disappointments, just the whole human element," Kostacopoulos said.

Harris was attempting to become only the second graduate of the Naval Academy to play in the major leagues. The first, Nemo Gaines, pitched in four games for the Washington Senators in 1921.

There are two other Navy products currently in the minors, but their situation differs greatly from Harris'. Pitchers Oliver Drake, with Baltimore, and Preston Gainey, with Milwaukee, both left the Academy as draft-eligible sophomores, before their five-year military obligation kicked in.

"The baseball guy in me of 30 years says it's almost impossible to sit out for five years and do this," Kostacopoulos said. "But the personal side of me says this kid has amazing talent and if there is going to be a guy, it might be this guy."

On April 20, Harris did become the guy. Mike Shildt called him down to the lobby of the hotel in Round Rock, Texas, where Memphis was playing, to tell him he would be joining the big-league team in Washington, D.C., the next day.

Harris was told his stay might not be long—outfielder Peter Bourjos was going on paternity leave—but that didn't matter. Harris knew he was being promoted because the Cardinals believed he was ready for the major leagues, not simply because of "his story."

In the fifth inning of the Cardinals' April 25 game in Milwaukee, Harris came in from the bullpen in relief of Wainwright, who had torn his Achillies tendon in the fourth while batting, an injury that would force Wainwright to miss the rest of the season.

Harris struck out the first batter he faced, Adam Lind, and pitched 1⅓ scoreless innings in his major-league debut. He pitched in 15 more games before he was optioned back to Memphis in June, the precursor to more trips up and down Interstate 55 the rest of the season, which is what usually happens to players trying to make that transition to the majors.

One of the realities of being in that situation, Harris soon learned, was having to deal with the logistics of life.

He got an apartment in St. Louis, which he kept even after returning to Memphis. The new truck he bought after the transmission gave out in his old one also remained in St. Louis, and by the end of the summer, Harris was back in the city as well.

"This year was a big year of just gaining experience," he said. "You go up, you go back down, you learn what you have to do to stay (in the majors). That's the next big step. You realize you have gotten there, now how do you get there and stay? I know what I have to do to improve."

The instruction and advice he got from coaches at both the major-league and Triple A levels, Harris said, demonstrated to him how close he was to becoming a reliable member of the Cardinals bullpen.

Harris never expected his transition from being a minor-league pitcher to a major-leaguer would be easy. In that respect, he really is no different than anybody in a similar position. He does appreciate the faith and patience the Cardinals organization showed in him, in believing in him, in giving him a chance.

"Nothing in this journey has been easy," he said. "My learning curve is much shorter and quicker than everybody else. I haven't had the time and experience in the minor leagues to improve."

Being told he was going back to Memphis, while disappointing, also inspired Harris to work even harder.

"It is probably the worst feeling you can imagine," Harris said. "You are so excited to be up there and no one wants to come back down. It's a terrible feeling, but it's also a huge motivator because you know what it's like up there and you want to be up there for good."

At every step along his journey, Harris knew he had a countless number of people rooting for him—those he went to school with, those he served with on active duty, all of those under his command who he encouraged during tough times to not give up on their own dreams.

Harris' story is their story. He hears from a lot of them on Facebook, wishing him well. He knows they are watching from places near and far.

When he and pitcher Marco Gonzales were both at Double A Springfield in 2014, they shared adjacent lockers. They shared bus rides and long conversations.

Gonzales made it to the major leagues shortly thereafter, barely a year after he was in college. Even though he knows Harris well, he doesn't know, nor can he imagine, everything his friend has gone through for more than 11 years.

"He's a natural-born leader," Gonzales said. "We believe in a lot of the same things. It's awesome what he is doing."

And what Harris is doing now is trying to write the perfect ending to his story.

"My only thoughts are to do my job, which is to come in and throw strikes and get guys out," Harris said. "If I can do that, that will get me to the big leagues. The guys who need to make that decision will make that decision.

"I had a really smart coach, Oliver Marmol (at State College) tell me one time that if you have a Plan B, your Plan A is probably not going to be too good. I loved that, and I've stuck with that. Right now my Plan A is to make it to the big leagues and I don't have a Plan B."

Cy Harris, thinking about what is to come for his son, can't help but think back to what he already has accomplished.

"Some of these guys haven't seen an eighth of what he's seen," Harris said. "They haven't been pushed to the brink. When he was first at the Academy they tried their best to get in his face. They had to push him to see what was in there. I told him, 'If they push you over there's no reaching back.' It was a mind game."

Harris has transferred much of what he learned at the Academy, and in his years of active duty, to his baseball life. Wearing a different uniform now, those memories will be with him forever.

Before every game at Roger Dean Stadium, before the National Anthem, the public address announcer asks for all active or retired military personnel to stand so they can be recognized.

"Every game, when they say that, he stands there and salutes and claps for everyone," Wainwright said. "The rest of us turn toward him and say, 'Thanks, dude.'"

5   TREY NIELSEN

WHILE MITCH HARRIS HAD TO WAIT CLOSE TO FIVE YEARS AFTER being drafted before he could begin his Cardinals career, Trey Nielsen thought his time with the organization was over after less than 24 hours.

That was how long it took after he got to Jupiter, Florida, for the Cardinals to tell him he had failed his physical and put him on a plane back home to Utah.

"The whole thing really took about three hours," Nielsen said. "I was home before the sun went down. It was kind of a long day."

Nielsen was the Cardinals' 30th-round pick in the 2013 draft after his junior season at the University of Utah. A converted infielder, Nielsen had only pitched six innings after injuring his arm about a week before the college season began. The injury was diagnosed as a partial tear of his ulnar collateral ligament.

Had he not been injured, Nielsen thinks he would have gone higher in the draft, but he still thought he was going to be fine when he showed up to take his physical and sign his contract.

"I knew my arm was hurt, but I was throwing," he said. "The doctor saw something else."

Luckily for Nielsen, he had a pretty good support system—with a good knowledge of baseball—waiting when his plane landed in Utah. Nielsen's father, Scott, pitched in the major leagues for four years with the New York Yankees and Chicago White Sox.

"Dad jumped on the phone and started talking with the area scout," Nielsen said. "Then we were in touch with Dan Kantrovitz, who talked to the GM (John Mozeliak), and about two weeks later I signed with the agreement that I would have Tommy John surgery. It all worked out.

"I had told them I was signable, that I wanted to play and would do whatever we had to do. We came up with the options. I think that my dad told them that regardless of what happened, if I signed with the Cardinals or went back to school, I was going to have the surgery. He brought that up to the Cardinals and we ended up agreeing on terms."

The surgery forced Nielsen to sit out the 2013 minor-league season, which made his professional debut in 2014 that much more special.

"In elementary school they always have those questions where the teacher asks what you want to be when you grow up, and I always said 'professional baseball player' because of my dad," Nielsen said. "That became more of a reality out of high school when I was drafted by the Cubs in the 42nd round, but I wanted to pursue a college career."

At that point, Nielsen really wasn't thinking about becoming a pitcher but those thoughts changed while he was in college.

"I loved hitting, but it was pretty apparent where my professional career was going to take me, and that was to the mound,"

Nielsen said. "I turned a lot of my focus toward pitching and I was doing well in the fall (of junior year) leading up to the season. It was just an unfortunate injury."

Both because of his relative inexperience as a pitcher and then sitting out all of 2013, Nielsen's career began without any fanfare.

"I was basically a third baseman who had Tommy John surgery and was drafted in the 30th round and given minimal money," Nielsen said. "The expectations for me weren't very high going into my career. I truly believe that. (The Cardinals) didn't know what they were going to get, and that made it easier for me to just go play.

"I knew what I had to do to have success. I took that approach. I stayed under the radar and worked hard. I played with minimal pressure, and it was really nice to go compete and show them what I could do and to have some success."

Nielsen began his first season with the State College Spikes in the bullpen but after seven appearances in which he was 3–0 with a 1.53 ERA, Nielsen moved into the starting rotation for the rest of the season. He was 0–2 with a 3.03 ERA, walking just 11 while striking out 31 in 32⅔ innings.

Nielsen also got to experience the thrill of winning a league championship as the Spikes won the New York–Penn League title.

Just as important in the long term, however, was Nielsen's conversion to the life of a professional baseball player.

"It's tough, to be honest with you," he said. "It's not a glamorous lifestyle. It's fun, and I love what I do, but there are days that are tough. It's a low pay grade and a very tedious schedule. If you can keep your mindset toward the end goal, that's what helps gets you through the days."

Nielsen believes that has been easier because of being in the Cardinals organization, and because of the advice he has gotten over the years from his father.

Nielsen was too young to ever see his dad pitch before Scott retired in 1991, but the two have talked frequently about the world of professional baseball.

"I was the youngest of four kids, and it was just getting tough for him to travel and be away from his family," Nielsen said. "So, he called it quits. He had a good job back home, too.

"I grew up around a high level of the game and with a good knowledge about the game, and that helped my baseball IQ and helped me learn the game at a quicker pace. My dad obviously has been through all of this, the ups and downs, and he always has advice when I need it. He definitely told me what to expect early on and he was spot-on. Things have changed a little bit since he played but the minor-league lifestyle is basically still the same."

Like most players in the organization, Nielsen does believe the Cardinals are different than other teams.

"I believe it's the structure," he said. "I talk to a lot of friends in other organizations and there just seems to be a better sense of structure here. There is a way the Cardinals go about things. They really focus on the little things and I think that adds up.

"We are constantly breaking down the game, whether it's in-game situations or backing up the bases. It's all about doing the little things right. Off the field I also think there is a sense of accountability to the Cardinals, to our families, to ourselves, and that we know we have to represent ourselves in a positive manner. That's really just what the organization emphasizes and that creates a family aspect and that's what you want in order to win. You've got to be together.

"I finally got my taste of the Cardinal way and it's pretty special, it really is. Once you buy into it and accept it, it's special."

Because his first season on the field was so successful, Nielsen came into the 2015 season hoping for similar results. He still was an under-the-radar prospect, especially when he opened the year in the rotation for the Palm Beach Cardinals with a former first-round pick, Rob Kaminsky, and the best prospect in the organization, Alex Reyes. He was joined about a month into the season by another former first-round pick, Luke Weaver.

While those higher-profile pitchers were getting all of the attention, Nielsen was left alone to do what he knew he needed to do.

"I just needed to play and continue to be on the mound," he said. "I had to adjust and learn. I took a couple of hard lessons and got hit around, but that's what I needed to progress. For me it's a feel thing. I made mistakes and I know how that feels.

"I have to break it down during my bullpen sessions and work on things. You always have to be progressing. I had to work off my failures and take the positives out of a bad game and work on the negatives."

There were not many negatives the first three months of the season. By the end of June Nielsen was 8–4 with a 1.85 ERA. Included in his starts was an outing on May 27 against Tampa in which he allowed just one hit and one unearned run in seven innings.

In an effort to limit his innings, Nielsen was moved to the Palm Beach bullpen in August, where he allowed only one earned run in 13⅓ innings covering six appearances, an ERA of 0.79. He struck out 11 while walking five.

Every day when the Palm Beach team was at home, Nielsen was in the same stadium where he had failed his physical, the same stadium where he had spent many long hours two years earlier going through the tedious rehab following his surgery, not knowing what the future held.

All of those experiences helped him, he realizes now, develop into the pitching prospect he has become—stealing some of the headlines away from his more heralded teammates.

"I did a couple of mechanical changes on my own (after the surgery) but it doesn't really change the way I pitch," he said. "My velocity returned. I still have that. I have really good command of my fastball, and this year I was able to throw both of my off-speed pitches for strikes. That's been a huge part of my development. I've been able to throw my changeup when I've been behind in the count.

"I think my ability to compete as a pitcher and command my pitches are my strengths."

It didn't take Nielsen long to realize that where he was drafted, and the fact he had to undergo surgery and missed an entire season before he ever threw a pitch as a professional, was not going to affect how the Cardinals viewed him when he did begin to play.

Being a prime draft pick, or a pick from the 30th round or later, or even being an undrafted player, whether that player is from a major university or a small college or high school, none of that matters as much as production.

That was a lesson Collin Radack was going to learn quickly as well.

6   COLLIN RADACK

LUCKILY FOR COLLIN RADACK, THE INAUSPICIOUS BEGINNING TO HIS professional baseball career was not an omen of things to come.

A few days after he was selected by the Cardinals in the 20th round of the amateur draft in 2014, Radack left his home in Austin, Texas, to join the State College Spikes in the New York–Penn League.

Radack already was nervous and unsure of what to expect, having been picked by the Cardinals after his senior year at Hendrix College, an NCAA Division III school of 1,500 students in Conway, Arkansas—and that was before he learned his flight had been canceled.

He and pitcher Austin Gomber, a fellow draftee also headed to State College, met when they found themselves stranded overnight at O'Hare Airport in Chicago.

"We left the terminal to try to find a hotel room but all of the hotels were booked," Radack said. "We couldn't get back in the terminal, so we ended up sleeping in baggage claim. I just wanted a bed to sleep in. I was tired, and I was worried because I was missing practice."

Radack caught a 6:00 AM flight to Philadelphia, where he spent several more hours in the airport before finally arriving in State College. His career has remained on the go from the moment he landed.

After helping the Spikes win the league championship, Radack moved up to Class A Peoria in the Midwest League to start the 2015 season, and after only 37 games the outfielder was promoted again, to high Class A Palm Beach in the Florida State League.

"It's been awesome," Radack said. "It's a learning process. I'm not trying to be a good minor-league hitter, I'm trying to be a good major-league hitter. Every day when I do well I ask my-self, 'What did I learn?' and when I fail, I want to know, 'What can I learn to take into the next day?'"

Peoria manager Joe Kruzel was more than pleased with the 23-year-old Radack's performance and knew he was ready for the promotion, less than two months into the season. He hit .293 for the Chiefs with two home runs and 20 RBIs.

"He's a big strong kid, he runs really well, and is good in the outfield," Kruzel said. "He has a good arm and is accurate. There are a lot of things to like."

Kruzel is not the only one in the Cardinals organization who feels that way.

Nobody had more confidence in Radack's ability as a college player than area scout Dirk Kinney, who tried his best to hide his affection for Radack from scouts for other organizations, something which is increasingly hard to do in the modern world where there are very few secrets among that fraternity.

A former college coach in Arkansas, Kinney maintained good relationships with the coaches in the state after becom-ing a scout. He had heard about Radack from another player in the organization he had signed the previous year, pitcher Blake McKnight, who had been roommates with Radack in the summer of 2012 when they played for the Athletes in Action team in the Great Lakes League.

Kinney and supervisor Mike Roberts were heading to a game to see a high school player and had to pass through Conway, so he called coach Neil Groat, who he used to work with running summer camps, and made arrangements to stop and put Radack through a workout.

"He took his last swing and ran to first, and I saw both of them look down at their stopwatches and then look at each other," Groat said. "They said, 'Can you do that again?' Like, 'Were we both wrong?' He is just a special athlete."

Kinney and Roberts came back to see Radack in a game, and they were hooked.

"We were joking about who would think we would find this kid at Hendrix College over a high school kid who was supposed to be really good," Kinney said. "Mike and I decided to keep this one to ourselves and not tell anybody.

"Was he the priority of the day when that day started? No. After seeing him, he turned into a priority really fast."

The Cardinals invited Radack to their pre-draft workout in Houston, where he put on another eye-popping display in front of Dan Kantrovitz, then the team's scouting director.

"It was extremely hard for me not to slip and say this kid's name," Kinney said of the 6-foot-3, 210-pound right-handed hitter. "He had legit tools for a big-leaguer across the board. There was nothing he couldn't do.

"It's hard to tell your boss that this guy has a chance to go to the big leagues as a D3 senior, and to Kantrovitz's credit, he didn't think I was too crazy. A majority of scouting directors would tell me I was full of it."

The Cardinals, of course, have had more than their share of success in recent years selecting players from small colleges. Kantrovitz and the Cardinals were able to look past the name on the front of the jersey and instead focus on the player's talent.

"I think you can find some really talented players who don't all play at Division I," Kruzel said. "He gets on base, he can steal a base, and he has a pretty good understanding of the strike zone. Usually the last thing that comes is power, and I think it's in there.

"He's starting to figure some things out and make some minor adjustments in his approach and swing. If he keeps moving in that direction you're looking at a young man who has the opportunity to play at some high levels."

Because Kinney was confident that he had seen more of Radack than others, he was comfortable telling Kantrovitz they could wait to take him until the 20th round.

"I told him if he had Texas on the front of his jersey he would have gone in the first five rounds," Kinney said. "There's no doubt in my mind. I knew no one knew who this kid was, so we waited."

The fact that Radack did not go to Texas or a similar school, and instead headed to Hendrix, probably had a lot to do with his development as the player who was so impressive to Kinney and Roberts.

While in high school, Radack was a member of the Austin Wings program, one of the premier summer travel prep teams in the country. Groat was then an assistant coach at Hendrix, and also worked in the school's admissions office.

A guidance counselor who worked with the Wings attended an event at Hendrix and told Groat she knew somebody who she thought would be a good fit for the school. Groat followed up on the lead, and soon Radack was headed to Hendrix.

"He just kind of fell through the cracks," Groat said about why Radack did not draw more attention from larger schools. "He was a really good role player on some really good teams. He was probably the sixth- or seventh-best player, not because he was bad but because those first five were pretty darn good. He kind of slid under the radar.

"Everybody thinks you have to play Division I or at a high level to move on to professional baseball, but you just have to go to a place where you can thrive and do good. Kids sometimes make a decision to go to a smaller school so they can play right away. If he had gone to a bigger school he might have played 20 games as a freshman and maybe started by the time he was a junior. Instead he came to a small school and started 165 games in four years."

Radack, who was born in the San Francisco Bay area and grew up as a San Francisco Giants fan, re-discovered a love for baseball at Hendrix that he admits had waned a little bit while he was in high school.

"When I was little I had no doubt in my mind I was going to play professional baseball," Radack said. "In high school it kind of got away from me. I sort of lost confidence; I didn't think I was good enough to go play.

"I was kind of a late bloomer. I was a good player, and a smart player, but I didn't have the physical tools. I saw a lot of guys around me who did and I just thought, *I don't have a chance.* Then I started working hard instead of wondering why I didn't have those tools, and put in the work to develop them."

Radack said he added about 25 pounds after graduating from high school, when he decided it was time to get serious if he wanted to pursue a career in the sport.

"I used to play with a chip on my shoulder. Probably the first three years of college ball I was trying to prove people wrong, when people said I can't do this," Radack said. "It really motivated me. But at the end of the day, it didn't really satisfy me that much. It was kind of like, 'OK, that's cool, they're wrong, now what?'

"I just want to work hard every day to give myself a chance. Ultimately when my career is over I want to look myself in the mirror and say I gave it everything I've got and have no regrets."

There was one day, when Radack was a junior at Hendrix, that he wondered if his career had taken a dramatic turn for the worse. Playing a game against Berry College, he was on third base when the pitcher uncorked a wild pitch and Radack broke for home.

He didn't get there because the pitcher, Levi Austin, came off the mound and tackled Radack as he ran down the baseline. The video of the play made it to ESPN's *SportsCenter* and went viral on YouTube.

"There was no reason behind it," Radack said.

Radack broke his little finger on the play, and while he remained in the lineup, the injury made him change his swing. Scouts who had begun to notice him stopped coming to his games, and Radack went undrafted as a junior.

He headed to Alaska to again play for Athletes in Action over the summer, and knows now that maybe that play happened for a reason—that it was better for him to not be drafted and be able to go back to Hendrix for his senior season, where he completed his degree in business and economics.

Radack also left as the school's all-time leader in games, runs, hits, triples, and stolen bases. He also set a record with a 28-game hitting streak. As a senior he hit .401 and also did not commit an error in the outfield in 158 chances.

"I know if I had gotten drafted, I wouldn't have come back for my senior year and I wouldn't have met my fiancé, Holyn," Radack said. "Honestly, at that point I don't think I was ready for pro ball. I was still raw. That summer in Alaska was huge for me."

It also was potentially huge for the Cardinals.

Groat and his assistant coach, Jay Mattox, made the 515-mile, eight-hour drive north from Conway to Peoria in May of 2015 for their first chance to watch Radack play as a professional. They didn't tell Radack they were coming, wanting it to be a surprise when they showed up at Dozer Park.

They did it because of the thrill of seeing one of their former players now playing at the next level, but also because of the relationship they had built over the years with Radack.

"Honestly, he is the most wonderful person you would ever come across," Groat said. "He is so incredibly nice and conscientious and an incredibly hard worker. We spent the first couple of years trying to convince him he could be as good as he is. He was always talented but when he came back for his junior year, after playing in the Great Lakes league, he was just different. He had a new confidence about him.

"He was the kid you wanted every parent and every recruit to come in contact with. He was our best player but also our best ambassador. He was Hendrix College's male athlete of the year and was our conference's man of the year, which is based on academics and off-the-field work coupled with athletic achievement. He is just a terrific kid."

It did not take long for McKnight to find that out, either, when they became roommates while playing for the team in Xenia, Ohio, several summers ago. The two bonded, stayed in touch, and when Radack joined the organization, became roommates again at spring training and in Peoria, where they lived with the same host family.

"He's one of the best guys I have ever met," McKnight said. "One of the things I told Dirk when he asked me about him was that there wasn't going to be anybody who was going to out-work him, and that he was a smart guy. He hasn't changed."

Radack and McKnight were reunited for the second half of the 2015 season in Palm Beach, where after missing about three weeks with a hamstring injury, Radack hit .285 with one home run and 20 RBIs in 70 games in helping the team win the South Division second-half title and advance to the playoffs.

"I think the biggest thing I have learned so far is just having a plan at the plate," said Radack, who, like almost all college seniors, received a $1,000 signing bonus. "In college I could just go out there and hit and didn't have to think about it too much. In pro ball you really have to have a plan.

"I'm learning what I am good at and what I need to work on. The biggest thing is probably just consistency and my approach at the plate."

Groat spoke like a father when he said how proud he was of what Radack already had accomplished so early in his career.

"Neither Jay nor I have kids, but it kind of felt like that when we walked into the park and saw him on the field," he said. "I am very excited for him. He has worked hard to get to this point."

Radack had a few moments of doubt about how his first full season as a professional was going to go when, on his way from Texas to his first spring training, his flight was canceled—just like the previous year.

At least this time, however, Radack was able to get a hotel room instead of having to spend the night in the Houston airport.

"It was way better," he said.

7 DIRK KINNEY

SHORTLY BEFORE NOON ON APRIL 3, 2015, AREA SCOUT DIRK KINNEY was preparing to leave his home in Olathe, Kansas, and make another three-hour drive to Springfield, Missouri, to watch that night's game between Dallas Baptist and Missouri State.

It's a route Kinney can almost drive in his sleep after five years of scouting Missouri, Kansas, and Arkansas for the Cardinals. Between trips to Springfield and Fayetteville, Arkansas, alone, Kinney has put thousands of miles on his car the last few years.

One lesson Kinney has learned over those years is the importance of being flexible in his planning; he knows things can change on a moment's notice. As with almost all area scouts, especially those who don't live and work in Florida or California, Kinney has a Plan A for the day and the week and a Plan B, in case something—usually a rainout—gets in the way of his preferred schedule.

Kinney was thinking about that when he heard the ding of his computer, meaning there was a new e-mail in his inbox.

He clicked on the message, which was directed to the group of Midwest scouts:

MSU v DBU Tonight has been canceled DH starting at noon Saturday. Jon Harris will start the first game KG

Dealing with rainouts is a fact of life for scouts in the Midwest. Not wanting to waste the day, Kinney called the University of Missouri in Columbia to make sure the Tigers' game that night against Florida was still on. Assured that it was, Kinney quickly called Mike Roberts, one of the Cardinals' top scouting advisors, and made plans to pick him up on the way to Columbia instead of Springfield.

It wasn't but a few minutes later, however, when Kinney learned something was amiss. The e-mail, reportedly from Keith Guttin, the longtime coach at Missouri State, was a fake. The game had not been canceled.

"It was probably the most bizarre thing I have ever seen," Kinney said.

Kinney believes he knows what happened, and the reason behind the bogus e-mail, but neither he nor Guttin have been able to prove it. Their theory is that it was sent by a scout for another team who could not be at the game that night and wanted to distract other scouts from going to watch Harris, who at the time—correctly, as it turned out—was projected as a first-round pick.

The mystery is why that scout thought it necessary to keep other scouts from going to the game. It was certainly not going to be the last opportunity to watch Harris during the season. Kinney, and Roberts, just shook their head when they tried to put the story together. It was just one wacky episode in the world of amateur scouting, which Kinney has come to know very well in just a few short years.

The 38-year-old Kinney first thought he was going to be a player, and he did pitch in college and briefly in independent baseball, before Tommy John surgery sent him back to college in preparation for a likely career in coaching.

He had surgery on his elbow in 1999, before the procedure became commonplace in the game.

"The doctor told me it was the second time he had done the surgery, and I told him, 'I don't know if you should have told me that,'" Kinney said. "It wasn't then what it is now, where it seems like every kid in America gets it."

Knowing his playing career was over, and already having earned a degree in kinesiology, Kinney went back to school and earned another degree in computer science, thinking it would make him more marketable to high schools looking for something other than another history teacher.

Kinney soon landed a job as the baseball coach at Eudora High School just outside Kansas City and spent seven years there before he got a chance to move up to the college ranks and become the pitching coach at Ouachita Baptist University, a small school in Arkadelphia, Arkansas.

"We had a good run there and won a lot of games, and the head coach, Scott Norwood, was hired at Arkansas–Little Rock. Instead of staying and becoming a head coach at 30, I went with him," Kinney said.

It was while coaching at Little Rock that the scouting door first opened for Kinney.

Norwood had been suspended for a game at Troy University, so Kinney had to serve as the head coach for the day. The Cardinals' area scout covering Arkansas at the time, Matt Blood, called Kinney after the game.

"He knew I wanted out of Little Rock and said there was a possibility he might be moving to North Carolina," Kinney said. "He asked if I would be interested in becoming an area scout and staying in the area."

Kinney must have said yes, because it wasn't long before his telephone rang again and the caller identified himself as Jeff Luhnow, at the time the Cardinals' scouting director. The two quickly came to an agreement that allowed Kinney to start watching players with the understanding his responsibilities and territory could grow over time.

That was in 2010, and Kinney has thrived in the position ever since. Partly, that's because being a scout means voicing opinions about players that you watch, and Kinney is never shy about voicing his opinion.

He and Roberts, who has worked for the Cardinals for more than 40 years, have developed an especially close relationship.

"He is my second father," Kinney said. "I talk to him like three times a day. He is everybody's father in our organization. We argue and bicker like fathers and sons. He's been the glue of this organization for a long time."

Kinney and Roberts first met through another older scout, Larry Chase, who worked for the Mets when Kinney was coaching in Arkansas. Chase has since died, but made the connection to Roberts, who, after living for a long time in Kansas City, moved to Hot Springs and often accompanies Kinney on his scouting assignments in Arkansas.

Kinney believes the stability of having longtime employees such as Roberts and others in the scouting department is one of the strengths of the Cardinals organization.

"Our national guys are all older and have been in the game for a long time so they sort of command respect and you listen," Kinney said. "Then we have a lot of young guys with really bright minds. We have a wide mix of guys who played in the big leagues, or were college guys like me."

Kinney also points out that the team has fewer area scouts than many other organizations, which he believes is a plus.

"Too many opinions are bad opinions for me," Kinney said. "Everybody is going to see kids when they have a bad day."

One of the keys to a scout's success, Kinney has learned over the years, is the ability to evaluate players on more than just the results of one particular game or workout. He is looking for players he can get excited about. The words he uses most often are *passion* and *conviction*.

"You have to have passion," Kinney said. "You have to get excited for stuff. I'm learning something every day. Sitting with guys from other organizations, you hear better ways to describe a player. Mike (Roberts) taught me what a 'pie thrower' was. It's a way to describe a pitcher's arm action.

"It's like if you are literally holding a pie and you don't want the pie to tip over. That was literally how this kid we were watching was pitching. Mike and I were standing outside the car in a parking lot later and people driving by us probably thought we were nuts. We were going over deliveries. Mike is a 76-year-old left-hander who played against Stan Musial. And he still has good arm action."

Passion, Kinney knows, leads to conviction. There is no place to check off that box on the scouting reports that he fills out and turns in to the Cardinals' front office, but it is definitely a factor in his evaluation of players.

He had it when he first saw Collin Radack at Hendrix College in Arkansas before the 2014 draft.

"Conviction to me is when a scout basically says I will go

down swinging with this guy. It's when a scout says I want this guy with this pick. He is going to play in the big leagues," Kinney said. "Sometimes you hear scouts go, 'Well, I don't know,' in talking about a player. If the scout says that, I don't want that player. If the scout doesn't know, why should we draft him?

"If a scout says, 'Well, he was really good last summer but this spring his tools diminished,' why are we even talking about him in the first place? We have a lot of scouts with passion and a lot of mellow guys. It's the scouting director's job to judge the conviction each guy has. Some scouts have convictions about everybody they turn in and think they are all going to play in the big leagues and become All-Stars. That ticks other guys off because you know it's not true."

When the season begins every year, Kinney's goal is to find players he can get excited about, ones who make him want to pound the table in the draft war room and demand the Cardinals select them.

It was one of the reasons he was still in the stands at the Kansas junior college tournament as a game stretched close to 2:00 AM before a pitcher he wanted to see, a reliever, finally got into the game. It's the reason he has driven to so many out of the way places, following up on a tip that there was a player there he really should see.

Kinney began his scouting trips in February before the 2015 draft looking for players who excited him, and he quickly found one who fit that bill in Fayetteville, playing the outfield for the Razorbacks. At the time he got excited about Andrew Benintendi there was little buzz about the player who would go on to become the SEC Player of the Year and the seventh overall pick in the draft by the Red Sox, well before the Cardinals had a chance to select him.

"Early on everybody thought I was crazy because I was turning him in as a second-round guy," Kinney said. "They said, 'Dirk, he's 5-foot-10, maybe,' and I said 'He's the best 5-foot-10 I've ever had.' The last report I turned in said I would take him as the 15th player in the draft, and then I was told by the front office that I was too light on him. Two months earlier they thought I was too heavy on him."

That is one of the realities of life as an area scout. In the span of a couple of months in the spring of 2015, he saw nine games in Fayetteville, putting all of those miles on his 2010 Honda Accord—which has gone from having 35,000 miles when he bought it used two years ago to more than 110,000 after the 2015 draft—only to realize the Cardinals would not have a chance at getting a player he really liked and believed could one day become a star.

"Some scouts go through a whole year and don't get a player," Kinney said. "It sucks, but it's part of it. I've been blessed each year."

More often than not, Kinney's recommended players have come from smaller colleges or high schools. He has become adept at finding players, especially pitchers, who don't attract a lot of attention or draw many scouts to their games.

Three players who fall into that category from previous years are Lee Stoppelman, a left-handed reliever from Central Missouri, and right-handed relievers Chris Thomas (who Kinney signed as a non-drafted free agent) and Blake McKnight. Kinney found both of the right-handers at small NAIA schools—Thomas at Avila University in Kansas City and McKnight at Evangel University in Springfield.

"You can find some pretty good seniors in the Midwest who haven't been viewed very much," Kinney said. "Kansas alone has 40 college institutions that have baseball—the bigger schools, plus schools in the KCAC, the HAC, and junior colleges."

Kinney knows it is his job to not miss on players from his territory. He has been wrong before about players, as has every scout, but not from a lack of effort. His background as a college coach has allowed him to develop good relationships with coaches in his region, who will be honest with him when he asks for their opinion about a player.

That background helps shape Kinney's final analysis of whether to recommend the Cardinals draft a particular player, and where he would rank him in the draft, or whether the team could wait and sign the player as a free agent.

It's the reason he logs so many miles driving each year, taking him on trips such as the time he drove from Kansas City to Conway, Arkansas, picking up Roberts in Hot Springs, to Arkadelphia, to Star City, back to Hot Springs to drop Mike off, then back to Little Rock—all in one day.

"That day we saw games in Conway, Arkadelphia, and Star City," Kinney said. "Legitimate guys that I saw that day which I turned in? Three."

That day was in 2014, and one of those three players was left-handed pitcher Davis Ward, from Ouachita Baptist, who was picked by the Cardinals on the final pick of the draft.

"Mike and I have been through some wild trips together," Kinney said. "He knows every out of the way burger joint anywhere. We have been through tornado warnings."

Roberts wasn't with Kinney when he twice had rental cars run out of oil in 2015, or when he blew a tire on a rental car only to find out the car was missing all of the pieces of the jack, and there was no shoulder on the highway. He had another incident where he blew a tire when he hit a pothole, then 30 minutes later, had the spare tire blow out while driving on the Kansas Turnpike in the middle of the night, forcing him to spend two hours sitting on the side of the road waiting for a tow truck to arrive.

"A lot more things go into this job than just driving and showing up at a game," Kinney said. "When you are doing pro coverage, your day consists of waking up in the morning, sitting in front of a laptop for five hours writing reports, maybe getting a workout in, getting to the game on time to watch batting practice, then the game, going usually to a cheap place to get something to eat, then waking up and doing it all over again the next day."

Those long days, and time spent on the road and in hotel rooms, can be hard on a family. Kinney and his wife were married in 2007, when he was still working as a college coach. Their jobs kept them living in separate cities for much of the first three years of their marriage. She now works as an advertising account director in Kansas City and they have a two-year-old son, who often cries when he realizes his dad isn't home.

When the baby was born in 2012, he spent the first three weeks of his life in intensive care, a difficult time for both Kinney and his wife.

"You are gone a lot in this job and you have to have a family with a lot of patience," Kinney said. "When your child is crying his eyes out because you're not home and you are not going to be home for a while, that's tough."

What gets Kinney through those moments is his love of his job, and the love of never knowing what each day is going to bring, especially in the months leading up to the three days which are like Christmas morning for every scout: the annual amateur draft in June.

After all of the trips he took throughout his three states before the 2015 draft, Kinney turned in favorable recommendations on 42 players. The Cardinals ended up drafting three of them—left-handed pitcher Jacob Schlesener from Logan-Rogersville High School, near Springfield, in the 12th round; left-handed pitcher Chandler Hawkins from Arkansas State in the 33rd round; and shortstop Joey Hawkins from Missouri State in the 40th and final round. The team signed one more of Kinney's guys, left-handed pitcher Brady Bowen from Friends University in Wichita, as a free agent after the draft.

As happens every year, there were players Kinney liked who did not wind up being picked by the Cardinals for one reason or another. One player who a lot of fans wanted to see selected was Missouri State outfielder Tate Matheny, the son of Cardinals manager Mike Matheny.

Because the team had drafted Matheny out of high school, if they wanted to pick him again, they had to get him to sign what is called a re-select card. If the player does not give his approval, the team that selected him in a previous draft cannot pick him again.

"The commissioner's office didn't approve Tate's card," Kinney said. "The family was uncertain about whether they wanted the Cardinals to draft Tate again, but two weeks before the draft they said it would be OK. Tate thought I talked to his dad once a week, and I had to tell him I had talked to him once in my life. The second time I had to get him to fill out the card I had to pull him out of the hot tub at the Missouri Valley Conference tournament.

"We wouldn't have been able to have a magnet on the wall for Tate if he had not signed the form, and Mr. DeWitt would have been like, 'Who is in charge of Missouri that didn't have Tate sign the form?'"

Matheny ended up going to the Red Sox in the fourth round.

In the days leading up to the draft, everyone in the scouting department comes together in St. Louis to make their final presentations and rank all of the available players on a large board so there are no surprises or mistakes when the draft gets underway—everybody knows exactly what the team is going to do.

On the morning of the first day of the draft, Kinney found himself in the emergency room of a local hospital. He had developed a rash for an unknown reason, and it gradually had been getting worse since he had been in St. Louis.

"I had thrown batting practice at our pre-draft workout the day before wearing sleeves because I didn't want anybody to see my arms," Kinney said. "It was awful. It was like 98 degrees out there. I was just starting to get very uncomfortable. Nobody knew I went to the hospital.

"I was really stressed out. I was pacing like I was a Nascar driver. I was walking in circles because I didn't know if I would be late to the meetings and I didn't want anybody to know about my allergic reaction. They thought I might have brushed up against a tree, but I said I was downtown—there were no trees. The doctors gave me some stuff to treat it. I hope that never happens again."

Kinney was able to get back to the war room before the day's first meeting and made it through the draft without any further incident, watching as scouting director Chris Correa turned in the cards for the three players from his area.

Kinney had put a lot of time and effort into scouting each of the three. He first saw Schlesener the previous summer and then saw him start three games during the school's spring season. A regional cross-checker saw him, as did one of the national cross-checkers, plus Roberts.

"We had five different guys see him, and then he came to St. Louis for the workout," Kinney said. "He touched 93-mph, but he didn't repeat his delivery at all. I knew his command was going to take work but he was raw enough and athletic enough that I thought it could happen. He had a big arm. Combined we were able to see almost every start he made in the spring."

Kinney didn't know if the Cardinals would be able to sign him, since Schlesener had the leverage of a scholarship to Arkansas and wanted a significant amount of money. As the days passed after the draft, however, Kinney became more convinced that Schlesener would sign, and he did.

"Some kids are better off starting as pro out of high school," he said. "Some kids should go to school. There was a possibility Schlesener would not have pitched much as a freshman at Arkansas because he doesn't yet have enough fastball command. They need to win games. With us he can take his time and work on his delivery and can get stronger. The kid doesn't even shave yet."

Scouting and evaluating players such as Schlesener illustrates how much the process has changed in just the few years Kinney has been doing it.

"When I started we just looked at pure stuff," Kinney said. "I didn't worry about a guy's delivery as much as I do now. Our guys can predict arm troubles as well as anybody in the business. I was told to let those guys do their grades, you grade the stuff, and we will put it together. Being a former pitcher, and a guy who has been cut on a couple of times, I can't help but look at a guy's delivery."

Improved technology also has changed the way Kinney scouts. Video, specifically slowing it down and enhancing it, allows scouts to get a closer look at a pitcher's arm action and delivery.

As far as evaluating hitters, the biggest change has been the importance of grading bat speed, Kinney said. Hitters at all levels produce good numbers because of good barrel control. "They can flick the bat and get a hit and get on base," Kinney said, "but they are not going to be able to do that against guys with more velocity. I didn't pay that much attention to bat speed when I first started. I just wanted to know if a kid could hit or not."

Kinney also has come to learn over the years that everybody thinks he can be a scout, but they want to get the job without first paying their dues. It wasn't that long ago that Kinney was managing the Edenton Steamers in the Coastal Plains college summer league in Elizabeth City, North Carolina, having to also work as the team's clubhouse attendant and spend part of each day washing the team's uniforms.

Kinney had two rules for his players on that team—play hard and don't do anything to embarrass the town. His team won the league championship. He already had been hired by Luhnow as a scout for the Cardinals, and did double duty that summer coaching as well as evaluating the players in the league as one of his first assignments.

"I know there are 958 people who would apply for my job if I quit who think they could do it and really have no idea what goes into this," he said. "Everybody thinks it's just going to games. That's the relaxing part of it. They don't see the 900 pieces of paper scattered across two beds in a hotel room in Kingsport, Tennessee, writing reports on Team USA players."

The unseen part of the job also includes the episodes where a lost Internet connection means having to rewrite a report, not to mention the problems with rental cars, or poor meals in out of the way restaurants, or getting lost on the way to a game, or driving for five hours only to have a popup storm cancel a game.

It's all part of the job, and Kinney loves it.

"You have to get excited for stuff," he said. "I saw a kid in an Appalachian League game that I would do backflips for. That stuff gets me excited. If it doesn't, you need to quit."

8   DEREK GIBSON

ABOUT A WEEK AFTER THE 2014 BASEBALL DRAFT, DEREK GIBSON, A recent graduate of Southeast Missouri State, got in his car and drove from his home in Bonne Terre, Missouri, to St. Louis in search of a job.

He parked his 2007 Chrysler Sebring outside of Busch Stadium, grabbed the sheet of information his father, Dave, had helped him prepare, took a deep breath, and walked inside the Cardinals' offices.

"The security guard asked if I had an appointment, and when I said no, he said I could just leave the paper there," Gibson said. "I said, 'Is there any way you can get somebody down here that I can talk to? I came from a long way away and really want to talk to somebody.' He called Dan Kantrovitz (then the scouting director) and he said to just leave the paper there."

Gibson was persistent, and finally Jared Odom, an assistant in the scouting office, came downstairs and talked to Gibson for five minutes.

By the time he walked back to his car, Gibson said, his cell phone had buzzed with an incoming e-mail. It was from

Kantrovitz, letting him know the Cardinals would evaluate his information.

"I can remember sitting there and looking at the stadium and thinking, *This is a really, really long shot*," Gibson said, "but it's the only time in my lifetime I will ever be able to do this. I thought, *I don't ever want to drive through St. Louis again and know I didn't give it a shot*."

On paper, Gibson knew, his baseball statistics were pretty impressive. He was coming off a .403 season as a senior at the Cape Girardeau school that included six home runs, 70 RBIs, and nine stolen bases in 57 games. He struck out just 21 times in 226 at-bats.

That was the last of his three years as a regular outfielder at Southeast, where he had originally gone to play quarterback on the football team. Gibson walked onto the baseball team and hit .338 as a redshirt sophomore and .332 as a junior.

Despite that performance and a long list of accolades and awards, the three-day baseball draft came and went without Gibson hearing his name called. A total of 1,215 players were selected in the draft and it came as a big surprise to Gibson that he was not one of them.

"I was upset," Gibson said. "It was a tough time. It was one of those times when you didn't really know where to go. I thought I was out of options. I just really thought I could play and could do something in the minor leagues and compete."

Gibson's father, a transportation manager for Anheuser-Busch, helped prepare the resume Gibson took with him to Busch Stadium, where the two, along with Gibson's brother, had gone to as many as 15 games a year while he was growing up.

"I thought, *My chances here are really slim*," Gibson said.

"But I also thought I had nothing to lose at that point. All they were going to do was tell me no."

Even though the Cardinals were Gibson's favorite team, he and his father didn't want to eliminate other options of landing a minor-league contract. So, three days after his stop at Busch Stadium, Gibson was back in his car on his way to Chicago, where he dropped off his resume with the Chicago Cubs and White Sox, then headed north to Milwaukee to visit the Brewers.

He spent the night at a motel in Kenosha, Wisconsin, and wondered if he should take his degree in biomedical science and apply to dental school.

"I just thought, *I need to go home,*" said Gibson. "*I'm wasting my time and spinning my wheels. It's impossible; it's not going to be. It's not meant to happen for me to play professional baseball. If I was going to play somebody would have signed me by now.*

"I told my dad, 'I think I'm going to come home tomorrow.' He wanted me to keep going on to Cleveland, Detroit, and Cincinnati. He told me to go on and hit those teams."

Gibson had not heard from the Cardinals since the e-mail from Kantrovitz, but he did get a call back from the White Sox, who asked if he could come in for a visit the next morning, which he did.

"I talked to a guy for about five minutes and as I was walking away from the offices, my phone rang," Gibson said. "It was a 314 area code but I didn't recognize the number. I answered the call and it was Dan.

"He asked me what I was doing. I didn't want to tell him I was in Chicago. He said, 'We've got a spot for you on our GCL team.' I was so pumped. He told me I was flying out to West Palm Beach at 7:00 in the morning."

As excited as he was, Gibson also immediately recognized the reality that he was seven hours away from home. He had to make the drive, pack, and get to the St. Louis airport in time for the early morning flight. His first phone call was to his dad.

"He was on cloud nine," Gibson said. "He's one of those guys who doesn't get excited about a whole lot. He is really level-headed, but he was extremely excited. That was the coolest moment.

"If not for my dad I wouldn't be sitting here today. He has pushed me through those tough times when I couldn't do it by myself. Every time I have a tough game or if I have a tough stretch, he picks me up. He is my rock."

Gibson made it in time for his flight, then passed his physical and signed his contract when he got to Jupiter—and received a check for $1,000 as his signing bonus. He used it to buy a Winchester shotgun.

The following day, June 20, Gibson found himself batting eighth and playing left field for the Gulf Coast League Cardinals. Even though he went hitless in four at-bats, getting an RBI because of an error, one fact outshined everything else—Gibson was now a professional baseball player.

Gibson played in 42 games for the rookie league team, hitting .301 with two homers and 22 RBIs. He played in two games for the Class A Palm Beach Cardinals, going 5-for-8, before the season ended.

Gibson did that despite playing with a bad hip, which required off-season surgery. Following about six months of rehab, he began his 2015 season in Palm Beach, making his season debut on June 2. After just 26 games with the team, in which he hit .376, he found himself called into manager Oliver Marmol's office.

"He said I was going to Double A and I couldn't believe it," Gibson said. "I didn't dream they would send me up here this fast."

Gibson got off to a slow start with the Springfield Cardinals, going 6-for-34 in 12 games. With Anthony Garcia rejoining the team following the completion of the Pan Am Games, where he played for his native Puerto Rico, Gibson was reassigned to Palm Beach.

The move did not discourage him.

"It was great to experience the next level for a few games and it made me a better player, without a doubt," Gibson said. "I am very aware of what it takes to be successful there and am going to do everything I can to finish this year out strong and make a push for a league championship with my guys."

Gibson had the same reaction only a few weeks later when he found out he was switching teams again, this time going down a level to the low Class A Peoria Chiefs.

"I think it's just part of being a free agent, you have to go where there's a spot, when somebody needs to fill a hole here or there," Gibson said. "It's tough at first when you get moved around. When you stay somewhere for a while you can get settled in. I'd really like to get to a point where I settle in at one spot but it's not always the way you want it to be."

Gibson had more success in Palm Beach and Peoria than he did in Springfield, hitting .320 in a combined 175 at-bats.

"There is an adjustment you have to make at each level," Gibson said. "The velocity on the fastball is less here. If you are going to be a good hitter, it's something you have to adjust to. When you go to Springfield the velocity goes up a little bit. When you go back to Palm Beach it goes down. That is always a challenge.

"No matter what team I've been on I have just tried to help us win. It's been a long year, and it's not easy. You just try to do the best you can every single day. You don't want to ever look back and have any regrets. It's easy when you know you gave it everything you had."

Gibson has gotten past the stage where reality meets fantasy of life in the low levels of the minor leagues, and is now able to concentrate on what he has to do to be successful.

"A lot of times (in 2014) I was half shocked I was there," he said. "It seemed like a dream. It seemed like I spent half of the time trying to play and half trying to set that dream aside so I could just play. Last year I went through a phase where I really couldn't believe I was here.

"I think I've done a better job this year of setting all of those emotional feelings aside and getting back to playing good hard baseball and being the best player I can be every day."

Gibson got to Springfield on July 4, just in time for one of the true joys of life in the Texas League: the 14-hour, 825-mile bus ride to San Antonio and Corpus Christi. He made it back to town for the start of a homestand on July 15, where he had a welcoming crowd waiting for him that included not only family members who had made the three-hour drive from Bonne Terre to Springfield, but also two youth teams from his hometown who just happened to be in Springfield.

The Cardinals allowed both the high school and under-10 teams to come into the stadium to watch batting practice and visit with Gibson.

Going back to Palm Beach and then down again to Peoria only made Gibson more determined to do what he needed to do to start moving back up the Cardinals' organization ladder.

"You just have to do whatever you can wherever you are that day," he said. "It's kind of the nature of the beast. Baseball can change in the blink of an eye. You never know what's going to happen next."

9   BRIAN HOPKINS

FROM THE FIRST TIME SCOUT BRIAN HOPKINS SAW NICK PLUMMER in center field and at the plate, he knew Plummer was a player he would like to see in the Cardinals organization.

It was in the summer of 2014, and Hopkins—the team's cross-checker for the northeast section of the country—was one of several Cardinals scouts attending the annual East Coast Pro Showcase in Syracuse, New York.

The tournament, run by scouts, brings together the best high school players from the eastern half of the country, giving scouts a chance to see how they perform against quality competition.

Hopkins has been attending the event every year since 2005, but as he analyzed what he had witnessed over the course of four days from Plummer, he was impressed with what he had seen.

"I don't remember any hitter ever being in the zone for as long as Nick was," Hopkins said. "He was squaring balls up all over the place. I liked his bat control, the consistent hard contact, how he played the game, the tools, the strength, the speed, and the way he played center field."

It was more than 10 months before the 2015 amateur draft, but Plummer's performance and the tools that he showed, one day before his 18th birthday, made him a player Hopkins wanted to see again.

He was the reason Hopkins found himself battling snow flurries and freezing temperatures on April 22 in the Detroit suburbs, getting another look at the Brother Rice High School star. Hopkins even took a picture of the poor weather conditions on his cell phone so he could show his fellow scouts from warmer climates some of the obstacles he had to face when they joke around about the drastic differences in scouting conditions around the country.

"What definitely stood out to me that day was that he was playing like it was normal weather conditions," Hopkins said. "He didn't bat an eye, he wasn't doing anything different, even though everyone else was literally shivering.

"What I saw from Nick was that he was such an even-keel guy and always seemed to have the same mentality, no matter if he was having a good day or a bad day, or if it was snowing. His mindset was very impressive. It would not have been a red flag by any means if he had been affected by the weather; it almost would have been expected."

The baseball draft always is an unpredictable event, especially for a team like the Cardinals, who have not been among the teams picking at the top of the draft for a long time because of their success. The team had the 23rd overall pick, and it was not a given that Plummer would still be on the board. As it turned out, he was, and the Cardinals called his name.

Before the night was over, they had also drafted another

player who Hopkins saw on that showcase team, a young third baseman from Brentwood, Tennessee, Bryce Denton, with the 66th overall pick in the draft.

Denton had stood out to Hopkins as well, not only in the East Coast Showcase but on the three occasions he saw Denton play for his high school in the spring.

"I liked him a lot regardless of his age, but theoretically he could have been a 2016 prospect," Hopkins said. "He was 16 when the event started. He turned 17 a few days later. He just consistently made hard contact. He hit the ball hard a lot. It just sounded different coming off his bat."

Being able to watch players such as Plummer and Denton—and play a role in them becoming members of the Cardinals—is something the 39-year-old Hopkins could only dream about not all that long ago.

Hopkins was a student at Elon College, now Elon University, in North Carolina majoring in sports management when the teacher in one of his first classes tried to warn the students about the long odds they faced trying to get a job in the business.

"I remember the teacher saying, 'Everyone wants to work in professional sports, but to be honest with you, the likelihood of that happening is slim to none,'" Hopkins said. "I remember sitting there and thinking to myself, *I will work in professional sports.*"

Hopkins proved the teacher wrong, but his climb up the ladder to his current position with the Cardinals has been far from easy. It included unpaid internships, long commutes to work, and even stocking shelves at a grocery store on the overnight shift for minimum wage so he could work for free as an associate scout for the Astros.

As he reflects back on that history, Hopkins considers it all a part of paying his dues.

"When I walked on to the Elon baseball team I knew what I wanted my future to be," Hopkins said, knowing it was unlikely his future would be as a player. "I offered to catch even though I didn't have any experience at the position, just to get my foot in the door. Eventually I moved to my primary position, which was in the outfield."

A native of Towson, Maryland, Hopkins landed an internship with the Class A Frederick Keys in the summer of 1996, a 55-minute commute from his family's house. The next year, he sent his resume to 19 different people with the Orioles looking for another internship and got two responses, one in group sales and one in public relations. He took the PR job because it was closer to the baseball operations department.

"Whenever they needed help filing papers or whatever, I was the first volunteer," he said. "It gave me a chance to meet people."

After graduating in 1998, Hopkins came back to work for the Orioles—for free—for six months before an entry-level position opened in the scouting department when Matt Slater—also now in the Cardinals' front office—left Baltimore to take a job with the Dodgers.

"It was definitely the low end of the totem pole, but my desk was in the draft room and my main job was to set up the room and organize it for the draft," Hopkins said. "Once the draft was over I gathered information for the trade deadline, then the off-season. It was almost like I was in school, getting an education in baseball. I asked a lot of questions and I got a lot of answers from a lot of great baseball people. It was an awesome learning process."

One reality of the job, however, was that it took place behind a desk. The more time he spent in the job, the more Hopkins knew he wanted to be at games, to be one of the people writing scouting reports instead of just filing the reports from everybody else. So, at the age of 27, after five years with the Orioles, he took a major risk.

Hopkins moved to the Dallas area, where the Astros gave him a job as an associate scout, in 2004.

"I wasn't married and I didn't have any kids," he said. "At the time both of the Astros scouts who covered Texas lived in Houston, so I thought I could help them out a bit in the Dallas area. It's essentially a volunteer position. There are a fair amount of guys who start out that way."

Hopkins needed to be able to pay bills and eat, however, so he took a job at the local Kroger's in McKinney, Texas, stocking shelves at night, making minimum wage.

There were some nights when he wondered if he was doing the right thing.

"It was one of those things I thought about at 3:00 in the morning when I was stacking cans of Campbell's soup," Hopkins said. "I thought, *This is what I want to do, and this is what I have to do right now to do it.*"

Hopkins also spent part of that year selling memberships to a local athletic club so he would have time to go watch players such as Hunter Pence, Ben Zobrist, and a young catcher named J.R. Towles. He got to write his own scouting reports. He got to talk to other scouts and coaches.

One of the people he stayed in touch with was Bruce Manno, with whom he worked in Baltimore. Manno, a veteran executive for many different teams, also happened to be the father of the woman Hopkins was dating at the time, Amanda.

Manno had gone to work with the Cardinals, and he put Hopkins in touch with John Mozeliak, at the time the team's assistant general manager. The Cardinals had two area scouting positions open, one in Texas and one in the Great Lakes region.

"Mo said they would really like to get somebody with more experience to cover Texas, but would I be interested in the other job," Hopkins said. "I said absolutely."

Hopkins was on the move again, this time to Ohio. He worked that region as an area scout for nine years. Among his finds was first baseman Matt Adams from Slippery Rock University, and the Cardinals took a chance on him in the 23rd round in 2009.

"The area scout is the foundation of the game," Hopkins said. "My first year with the Cardinals I learned so much from a lot of different people, especially Mike Roberts, who was my first cross-checker. One of the things he told me was that I was going to build my database of players over the years and be able to compare guys and see what worked and what didn't work. I do that all the time now."

Hopkins also sought and received advice from the team's other scouts, especially those who covered surrounding states, people such as Mike Shildt, Scott Melvin, and Tommy Shields. Melvin and Shields now work for the Royals.

"You are always learning, and what Mike Roberts taught me that first year has been really true," Hopkins said. "I watch players now and think about a guy I saw in 2005 or 2009, and here's what I thought about him and here's what he's doing now. What can I learn from that? The database is always changing."

One of the players in that database who Hopkins thinks about often is Adams, who rose quickly through the minor-league

John Mozeliak became the 12th general manger in St. Louis Cardinals history in 2007 after the team parted ways with GM Walt Jocketty. (Bill Greenblatt/UPI)

Since 1986, Mark DeJohn has spent all but one season as a member of the Cardinals organization. For much of that time, he learned everything he could from the legendary George Kissell. (Allison Rhoades/Peoria Chiefs)

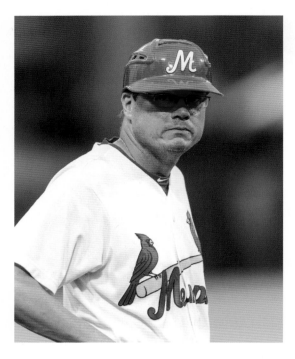

Mike Shildt spent three seasons as the manager of the Double A Springfield Cardinals before taking over Triple A Memphis in 2015. (Roger Cotton/ Memphis Redbirds)

After serving in the United States Navy, Mitch Harris became just the second graduate of the Naval Academy to appear in the major leagues, in 2015. (Roger Cotton/Memphis Redbirds)

A 30th-round pick in the 2013 draft, Trey Nielsen had to endure Tommy John surgery before beginning his career as a Cardinal. (Christopher Shannon/ State College Spikes)

Though other teams may have overlooked Collin Radack, a graduate of Division III Hendrix College, the Cardinals gave him every chance to succeed. (Allison Rhoades/Peoria Chiefs)

Dirk Kinney has spent hundreds of hours driving thousands of miles across the Midwest as an area scout for the Cardinals since 2010. (Dirk Kinney)

Derek Gibson's persistence and initiative helped land him a spot with the Gulf Coast League Cardinals in 2014. (Mark Harrell/Springfield Cardinals)

Brian Hopkins, now in his third season as a Cardinals scouting cross-checker, is responsible for the East Coast from Maine to South Carolina and from eastern Tennessee to Michigan. (Brian Hopkins)

Paul DeJong put his career in medicine on hold to pursue his dream of being a St. Louis Cardinal. (Allison Rhoades/Peoria Chiefs)

As the team's director of international operations, Moises Rodriguez (left) oversees 14 scouts who identify prospects from throughout Latin America. (Rob Rains)

Alex Reyes moved from his hometown in New Jersey to the Dominican Republic in order to maximize his chances of becoming a professional baseball player. The Cardinals signed him in 2012. (Mark Harrell/Springfield Cardinals)

Aledmys Diaz make the difficult decision to defect from Cuba in 2012 and joined the Cardinals organization in 2014. (Mark Harrell/Springfield Cardinals)

Cardinals director of pro personnel Matt Slater has traveled the world looking for new talent. (Matt Slater)

When he was nine years old, Jacob Wilson told his fourth-grade teacher he wanted to be a baseball player when he grew up. The Cardinals drafted him in 2012. (Roger Cotton/Memphis Redbirds)

Rowan Wick moved from the outfield to the pitching mound in 2015, a tactic the Cardinals have used successfully in the past. (Christopher Shannon/State College Spikes)

system en route to becoming the Cardinals' starting first baseman before a torn quad muscle forced him to miss most of the 2015 season.

"I thought he was going to be good but he has clearly exceeded expectations," Hopkins said. "I don't know if I ever saw him face better than 87 miles per hour pitching. I knew he had the bat speed and bat control, and was a hitter before he was a power hitter. Watching what he has done helps me with my database. He had that foundation to build on what he has done."

One reality which Hopkins and all scouts face is that they are not perfect. Sometimes they make mistakes in evaluating players. Sometimes players turn out better than the scout expected, sometimes worse. It's not always something the scout did wrong, however—the problem is often one that nobody could have predicted.

"'It's a humbling game' is a phrase that's used all the time by scouts," Hopkins said. "You are wrong more than you are right. One of the challenges of scouting in cold-weather areas is you often don't get to see a player very many times. You have to make quick decisions. You might only get one look at a guy—and then have to decide if you want to go and see him again.

"That's been a big part of my growth process. The window in the Northeast is so short, and as a cross-checker, we have a lot of guys area scouts want us to go see."

Hopkins wrote reports on more than 100 players before the 2015 draft. Sometimes he agreed with an area scout's evaluation, sometimes he didn't. He believes it is actually healthy when there are friendly disagreements about a player's ability and projections for the future.

"It's never personal," Hopkins said of those differences. "It's just my opinion. It's important to write reports on what you saw. Maybe the player didn't have a good day the one day I happened to be there. Maybe he had a great day. If I disagree with the area scout it's just because I saw something differently."

That was another lesson he got from Roberts and some of the other longtime scouts who have spent decades with the Cardinals. That continuity definitely has played a key role in the organization's success.

"I can't imagine if you talk to any scout from the Cardinals that they haven't learned something from Mike Roberts," Hopkins said. "He's been a valuable mentor to all of us, and especially to me."

Hopkins has learned a lot of lessons on his own over the years as well. One is how important it is to have a support system at home during the many nights and weeks he has to spend on the road.

He and Amanda ended up getting married, and because of her father's years in the business, she certainly understood what she was getting into.

The couple now have two boys, Carter, who turned four in the summer of 2015 when Hopkins was scouting the Cape Cod League, and Gavin, who was born January 2, 2015. In order to spend more time at home and less time in hotels, Hopkins moved his family from Ohio to North Carolina in 2014, but even that didn't happen without incident.

A week before the family sold their house in Ohio, the basement flooded. Hopkins naturally was out of town when it happened.

"Scouts who are married with kids will tell you that their

wife basically becomes a single mom for parts of the spring," Hopkins said. "She has a lot of responsibility. Having her dad in the game helped out because she kind of knew what the business was like, and having that understanding is vital. We talked about that all the time. We dated for several years before we got engaged and then got married. There were no surprises."

That might be true from a marital standpoint, but Hopkins does still get surprised all the time, and sometimes it has nothing to do with his job—except for the travel involved.

After the 2013 season, the Cardinals had organization meetings in Phoenix. Heading home afterward, Hopkins first had to fly to Chicago before going on to Cleveland.

"I always get the aisle seat but that day I decided to get a window seat because I was tired and I wanted to sleep," Hopkins said. "I fell asleep with my legs crossed and didn't think anything about it."

It was a couple of days later when Hopkins was in church that he began to feel something was wrong.

"I had a pain in my chest and I started sweating profusely," he remembered. "I was short of breath, and I had to leave church. My wife is now a nurse practitioner, and I called her to tell her about it and she told me to go directly to the emergency room.

"If she hadn't told me to do that I probably would have thought I was just getting sick and gone home. They ran a bunch of tests and the doctor came in and told me, 'I can't believe this but you've got a blood clot in your left lung.'"

Hopkins found out he had apparently developed the blood clot when he had his legs crossed on the flight.

"They said the clot can start out in your calf and go to your lung, and then break off and go to your brain," he said. "Potentially going to the emergency room could have saved my life. What they said was anytime you are in the car or plane for more than two or three hours, you need to get up and walk around.

"I've driven from Cleveland to Louisville, which is about five hours, multiple times without stopping, but I've never done it since. I always stop at a rest area and walk around, just for a few minutes."

Hopkins was on blood thinners for nine months, but luckily has never had any more problems. He used his experience as a warning for other scouts, who often log long hours behind the wheel of a car.

When he was an area scout, Hopkins drove an average of 47,000 miles a year, many times logging more than 8,000 miles in a month between March and May. Like all scouts, he has endured his share of car problems over the years. He remembers the time his alternator went out in Bowling Green, Kentucky, but thanks to the help of a scout who lived there, Earl Winn, he got it fixed without missing a pitch of the doubleheader he was there to see.

He was driving with Roberts in the spring of 2005 when the cylinder on his 2000 Mustang blew out on the Ohio Turnpike, forcing the scout to have to rent a car to continue their trip. Roberts still reminds Hopkins of that incident at least once a year and they laugh about it.

Better memories are those such as the day Hopkins returned a rental car back at the airport in Baltimore and saw the agent do a double take—he had driven more than 2,000 miles in just a matter of days.

One trip from the spring of 2015 was an example of what Hopkins and other scouts endure all the time.

"The weather was so bad that many high schools were still not even playing late in the spring because their fields were so saturated from all the snow and rain," he said. "I was going to a high school game in New York in the morning, then going to a game that afternoon in Pennsylvania. Then I was planning on seeing a kid in Maryland the next day, so I drove down to be in position the night before.

"I woke up in the morning and found out the game had been canceled. I contacted three area scouts to go over my different options—with the biggest factor not wanting to get rained out for several days in a row. Every day is valuable, especially when the window is so short."

Hopkins' best option for the next couple of days turned out to be in Charleston, South Carolina. Through the phone calls with Jason Bryans, Sean Moran, and Matt Blood, who is responsible for the Carolinas and half of Virginia, Hopkins found out he could see two players he wanted to see on the same trip, high school prospects Kep Brown and Trey Cabbage.

He booked a flight from Baltimore to Charleston for just $164—a good sign, he thought.

Ironically, Hopkins saw Brown, a promising power-hitting outfielder, two nights before he tore his Achilles tendon in a game. The Cardinals ended up selecting Brown in the 10th round, but were unable to convince him to sign. Brown was planning on going to the University of Miami, but just before the school year began, he switched to a junior college in South Carolina, making him eligible to be drafted again in 2016.

"On that trip I saw Brown and Trey Cabbage, who was from eastern Tennessee but was playing in South Carolina on spring break," Hopkins said. "I wondered then if we would end up drafting at least one of them because it was just fate that I got to see them. I originally was not going to be there."

Hopkins, now in his third season as a cross-checker, is responsible for the East Coast from Maine to South Carolina and from eastern Tennessee to Michigan.

"The area scouts essentially dictate my schedule because I am going to see players that they like," Hopkins said. "My life is dependent on the area scouts having a good feel for their area."

The Cardinals' area scouts in the northern states are both veterans, Bryans and Moran, and Hopkins trusts them and their ability to deal with the challenges of scouting in the cold-weather, short-window environment.

The sheer volume of players makes it impossible for a cross-checker to see all players in his area, which again puts the focus on the area scout when it comes to picking players in the later rounds of the draft, or even trying to sign players afterward who were not drafted.

Those are the types of success stories scouts such as Hopkins really appreciate.

One player who fell into that category for him was Zach Petrick.

In June 2012, Petrick, a right-handed pitcher, finished up his degree in business administration at the University of Northwestern Ohio, an NAIA school of 4,500 students in Lima, Ohio, that did not even have a baseball program until 2010. Petrick's dream was to play professional baseball, perhaps making it to the majors, as his older brother Billy had done for eight games with the Cubs in 2007 before injuries derailed his career.

He knew his best path to make that dream come true was through the draft, which was why he sat in his dorm room listening online as the 30 teams went through the 40 rounds of the draft, calling off the names of 1,238 players.

Petrick's name was not one of them.

"I was listening with my teammates, and to hear all of those names and not hear mine was pretty difficult for all of us," Petrick said. "I knew I still had something in the tank."

Two days later, Petrick was in his room packing his belongings, planning to head to a tryout with the Joliet Slammers of the independent Frontier League, near his hometown of Morris, Illinois, when he got a phone call that changed his future. Hopkins was on the other end of the phone, offering him a chance with the Cardinals.

Petrick has made the most of that chance. He went from being undrafted in 2012 to being named the organization's minor-league pitcher of the year in 2013. He was invited to major-league spring training the following year, and spent the 2015 season in the rotation at Memphis, after which his rights were transferred to the Yokohama DeNA BayStars.

Hopkins was happy for Petrick and how he progressed through the organization.

"One hundred and 10 percent of the credit goes to Zach," Hopkins said. "He took full advantage of the situation. It underlies everything we do as scouts. All we can do is give players an opportunity, and it is up to them to work to maximize their ability and take advantage of the opportunity that has been given to them. It's fun when you see guys do that."

The Cardinals were able to find out about Petrick in the fall of 2011. Some of the small schools in Indiana had organized a day for scouts to watch several players from those schools at the same location, but the schools in Ohio were not doing that.

"There are a lot of good small schools in Ohio and the window to see games there is so short because of the weather," Hopkins said. "I called some of the guys I knew at the schools and we got the players and scouts together and it was beneficial for everybody. It's a win-win when you can see a bunch of players in one location."

Petrick was one of the players at that showcase, and Hopkins flagged him as somebody he wanted to watch the following spring.

"I went and saw him as part of doubling up with another game in the area that day," Hopkins said. "I don't think he pitched very well that day, but he still stood out. His curve ball was the pitch I really noticed."

The 2012 draft was reduced from 50 rounds to 40, one of the reasons Petrick was not selected and was available to sign with the Cardinals as a free agent.

Deciding to organize that showcase for small-school players was another way Hopkins was working to build his database. So too were two other ideas, one of which was his, and one which came from the Cardinals.

In the summer of 2007, the Cardinals assigned several of their scouts to spend several days with one of the low-level minor-league affiliates, including putting on a uniform and sitting in the dugout during games. Hopkins went to Batavia in the New York-Penn League, where Mark DeJohn was the manager and Shildt was a position coach.

"It was just a great learning experience," Hopkins said, "especially for a guy like me who did not play professional baseball. It was great to see how guys handled themselves and to experience how the game was played at that level. I just sat on the bench and listened and learned.

"I've always tried to stay in touch with guys I signed and it's helpful to pick their brains. I ask them for advice to give to new guys just starting out. I remember telling Matt Adams when he was getting ready to report to Johnson City that one of the things he was going to have to deal with was handling failure. He had never really had to do that before. That is a big thing for every hitter.

"As it turned out, he hit .365 that year."

When he was in his second year as an area scout for the Cardinals, Hopkins organized and ran a scout team which played on weekends in the fall. He brought in high school players from Ohio, Michigan, and even western Pennsylvania and western New York to play against similar teams. Over the years kids from West Virginia and Kentucky also have played on the team. There have been a lot of talented players on that team over the years who have gone on to the majors, including Derek Dietrich, Travis Shaw, Matt Wisler, Daniel Fields, Andrew Chafin, and Matt Marksberry.

"I really liked doing it," Hopkins said. "One of the reasons I did it was so I could get to know the players on a personal level for my job, and I also enjoyed building relationships with them. I felt like it was something I could do to make a difference in the lives of other people. Many of these kids had played against each other on other teams, but they really came together quickly on this team in the fall because they all had the same goals and aspirations.

"As scouts we see the same situations every year and it's normal to us, but for kids and their parents going through it for the first time, sometimes it's a shock. Being able to have this team and being able to talk to kids and their parents about what to expect through the scouting process I hope was helpful and beneficial to them and prepared them for what was going to happen. I value the friendships and relationships I have built over the years with those players and their parents."

Nobody could be prepared for what happened to one of the players who came through Hopkins' team in 2011 and 2012. Left-handed pitcher Zach Farmer was an outstanding prospect who signed with Ohio State. He pitched for Hopkins in the fall of his junior year, but was not able to play as a senior because of an ankle injury.

Farmer pitched three innings in the game on September 10, 2011, and Hopkins kept the lineup card because it was also the first game Carter, his oldest son, had attended. He was going to show that card to Farmer on a family trip to Ohio in the summer of 2015 but he never got the chance. A week before the trip, Farmer died at the age of 21 from leukemia, which had been diagnosed when he was a freshman at Ohio State.

"He was awesome," Hopkins said. "He was soft-spoken but very competitive. He was a hard worker and just a great kid."

Getting to know players such as Famer, as well as Adams, Petrick, Plummer, Denton, and all of the others he has scouted and signed over the years is what Hopkins enjoys most about his job. Seeing players such as left-handed reliever Dean Kiekhefer, a 36th-round pick out of Louisville in 2010, make the Pacific Coast League All-Star team in 2015 is the kind of success that makes Hopkins smile.

"One of the things which has always been impressed upon me by people such as Mike Roberts is that we are always learning," Hopkins said. "We are always trying to be better. As scouts we are always looking for guys who can maximize their potential. That's one of the reasons I try to get to know their makeup as much as possible.

"What I want to do is be the best I can be. When we are on the road driving, away from our families and staying in hotels, you want to be doing the best job you can do. I don't want to look back and think I could have worked harder or done something different. We give players an opportunity, but as a scout I am very thankful for the opportunity I have and I want to make sure I am making the most of it."

10   PAUL DeJONG

THE DAY BEFORE THE AMATEUR DRAFT IN 2015, THE CARDINALS invited 25 players to a special workout at Busch Stadium, something they have been doing for several years.

Paul DeJong was one of the players invited, and he came—even though he could not participate in the workout because of a broken thumb, an injury suffered late in his season at Illinois State.

It was the first time DeJong had even been at Busch Stadium, and as he returned to his home in Antioch, Illinois, he was hoping it had not been a wasted trip—or would be the last time he was ever on the field at Busch Stadium.

"It was amazing. I was in awe," DeJong said. "The stadium was beautiful."

For the Cardinals, having DeJong make the effort to drive to St. Louis even though he was injured definitely was a factor when the team selected him in the draft's fourth round.

"I got to sit down and talk with him," said Chris Correa, the scouting director at the time, after making the selection. "He's a really bright kid. He could go to medical school if he wanted but he is ready to get his pro career started."

DeJong was a redshirt junior at Illinois State and had already completed his undergraduate degree in biochemistry, graduating with a 3.76 GPA in four years while also playing summer ball. Bo Durkac, his college coach, acknowledged, however, that it was DeJong's baseball ability which prompted the Cardinals to draft him.

"You've got to have the ability first," Durkac said. "Let's not paint him out to be a good guy who can't play at all. The guy can play.

"He's very polished, he's very mature. Talking to him is like talking to a college professor. On the field his biggest tool is his bat. He's got a really classic swing, very smooth. He generates a lot of bat speed and he can hit the ball a long way."

DeJong led the Missouri Valley Conference with 14 homers in the 2015 season, after hitting 20 to lead the summer Northwoods League in 2014. He also was second in that league with 61 RBIs.

It was his performance in the summer that convinced DeJong to put his plans to go to medical school on hold and pursue a baseball career. He was drafted by the Pittsburgh Pirates in the 38th round in 2014 before coming back for his fourth season with the Redbirds.

"It wasn't something I initially expected but definitely I saw it and worked for it," DeJong said. "I kind of approached (2014) as sort of a minor-league season practice, playing every day for 70-plus games. I think the success there kind of spilled over into the spring.

"At that point I knew this was going to be my goal—to come back so I could improve my draft stock. I'm excited to start the next phase in my life."

Durkac was not surprised at DeJong's success.

"If every player was like him college coaches would not have gray hairs," Durkac said. "We would not have any issues with behavior problems or issues in the classroom. He is the embodiment of everything a college student-athlete is supposed to be.

"When he first came here he wasn't a pro prospect in anybody's mind. When you have the success he had on the field, however, you start singing a different tune, and now he's all about baseball."

One of the biggest hits of DeJong's college career occurred during his junior year when he hit a grand slam to rally the Redbirds to a victory over rival Illinois.

"I've been working at both my mental game and my development at the plate," DeJong said. "I still have some work to do. I think I can go up from here."

DeJong certainly gave the Cardinals what they expected in his first pro season. Showing no ill effects from the broken thumb, he destroyed pitching in the rookie-level Appalachian League.

In 10 games, he was 18-for-37 with four home runs and 15 RBIs. That earned him a quick promotion to Class A Peoria, just 30 minutes from where DeJong had spent the last four years going to college in Normal.

Making it back onto the field in Peoria in July was not something DeJong had expected. He had been there for a three-game series against Missouri Valley rival Bradley just two months earlier.

"It's unbelievable to think I was just here in May," DeJong said. "It's been a whirlwind. It's been a wild adventure and I'm trying to enjoy every second of it."

The Illinois State dugout was the same one the Peoria Chiefs use at Dozer Field, on the first-base side of the field. On his way to their clubhouse, DeJong walked right past the door to the Chiefs' locker room.

"I saw the clubhouse and I thought maybe that could be me some day, but I never gave it too much thought," he said. "It's just been unbelievable."

DeJong's story is similar to that of several players the Cardinals have drafted out of Missouri State, which shares Hammons Field with the Double A Cardinals. DeJong has played games there too, since Missouri State is also a member of the Missouri Valley conference. Playing on a familiar field has helped ease some of the adjustments DeJong knew he would have to make from the college ranks to the professional game.

"In rookie ball there was a lot of talent and a lot of good arms," he said. "What I saw was a lot of raw pitching. At this level you see a lot more fine-tuned pitching, guys who can throw multiple pitches for strikes in every situation. I'm just trying to absorb all of the information and make the adjustments that I need to make."

Those adjustments came pretty easily, as DeJong hit .288 with five home runs and 26 RBIs in 56 games in helping lead the Chiefs to the Midwest League playoffs.

DeJong believes one of the biggest reasons for his success was being freed from the stress of not knowing what would happen in the draft. After playing multiple positions in college, he has settled in at third base for the Cardinals.

"The way I saw it once the draft was over, I didn't have to worry about who was watching from the stands, where was I going to go, all that kind of stuff," he said. "I could just go out and play. I couldn't keep up the success (at Johnson City) but to start out hot means everything. It kind of carried over for a period. Having confidence helps get you on the right track.

"My strengths as a player have carried over. I have weaknesses I need to improve on, to make myself a better player. But I think my skill set and attitude fit the Cardinals very well."

Like all players coming into the organization, DeJong had heard stories about "the Cardinal way" without really knowing what that meant. Now that he has been a part of the organization, even for less than a year, he has a better understanding.

"The more I am around the more I see it," he said. "We talk about it a lot. It's just the way we go about our business every day, always wearing red, things like that. I'm picking up on what the Cardinals are all about."

Just the fact that he is now a professional baseball player has taken some time to get used to, DeJong said.

"Every time you get asked for an autograph you kind of step back and think, *Wow, these kids want* my *autograph*," he said. "It's a cool experience. It's also nice to get paid and have money in the bank. That's not the real reason I am playing this game, but it makes it a little bit different.

"It's more about the opportunity to be able to play the game every day and have this for my job. I couldn't ask for anything better."

DeJong has had no second thoughts about putting a potential medical career on hold—maybe temporarily, maybe permanently.

"That was something I was considering before I knew I would have an opportunity to play professional baseball," DeJong said. "I'm going to take it as it goes. Right now I am focused on baseball. You have to think about both the mental and physical aspects of the game.

"The physical work starts in the off-season to prepare your body. I'm more focused now on the mental side of things. You have to hone in on every pitch of every at-bat. It's going to be a challenge to try to develop myself to be better at that."

DeJong was not the only player from that workout day at Busch who ended up with the Cardinals. Of the 25 players who were there, the Cardinals picked six of them in the draft, including DeJong.

Also selected, at least in part because of that workout, were Bryce Denton, Jacob Schlesener, Ryan Helsley, and Orlando Olivera, all of whom signed with the organization. Denton turned down a scholarship to Vanderbilt, and Schlesener one from Arkansas. The Cardinals also selected a high school catcher from Oklahoma who was at that workout, Josh Rolette, but he elected to go to Kansas State instead of signing.

While the Cardinals' scouts and officials got a chance to see those players merely by walking out of their offices, Moises Rodriguez can't see many of the players he goes to scout without leaving the country.

11   MOISES RODRIGUEZ

MOISES RODRIGUEZ CAN LOOK OUT THE WINDOW FROM HIS OFFICE onto the playing field of Roger Dean Stadium in Jupiter, Florida, but what he really sees is the world.

As the Cardinals' director of international operations, Rodriguez uses his office as the base from which he connects with 14 scouts who have helped the organization find and sign players from throughout Latin America, including the Dominican Republic, Venezuela, Panama, Colombia, Nicaragua, and Cuba.

Some of the organization's top prospects signed as international free agents, including current major-leaguer Carlos Martinez and prospects such as pitcher Alex Reyes, outfielder Magneuris Sierra, and shortstop Edmundo Sosa.

There are different rules for signing international players that make it far more competitive than selecting players through the amateur draft, which leaves players with only one choice—to sign with the team that drafted them or not sign.

International players, on the other hand, can receive offers from multiple teams and then sign where they wish. The teams do have a signing cap, similar to the amateur draft, which forces teams to decide if they want to allocate most of their available pool to one player or spread it around to multiple players.

"What's changed a little bit is your strategy, because your bonus pool is based on last year's major-league standings. So because we finished so high we have one of the smallest pools," Rodriguez said before the signing period began on July 2, 2015.

"I think we've been consistent that if we feel strongly about going after high talent we'll go after them, but at the same time, with limited pool space, we can't be maybe as aggressive as we could have been in the past with a guy like Carlos.

"The question becomes, does it make sense to go all in on one guy? Those are the sort of internal questions that we ask ourselves. It's sort of hard to go down that road when you have limited pool space."

The Cardinals' top international bonuses from 2014 went to right-handed pitcher Junior Fernandez—who, like Reyes, actually spent part of his youth in the United States—and to 16-year-old third baseman Elehuris Montero and 17-year-old shortstop Starlin Balbuena from the Dominican Republic.

Fernandez, now 18, was with the Gulf Coast League Cardinals in 2015 while Montero played for the organization's Dominican Summer League team based at their new training academy.

Of the 31 players on the rookie level GCL Cardinals in 2015, 13 were signed as international free agents, including 18-year-old outfielder Jonathan Rivera, signed in 2013 from Panama.

It's likely right-handed pitcher Alvaro Seijas will be pitching there soon, too. Seijas was the Cardinals' top signee in the international class in 2015, a 16-year-old from Maracay, Venezuela, who agreed to a $762,500 bonus. The Cardinals thought enough of Seijas to invite him to their Florida instructional league at the end of the 2015 season.

"He is a big-time arm and he's got stuff," Rodriguez said. "It's going to be fun."

The Cardinals had multiple scouts and officials evaluate Seijas, watching him pitch in three different countries, including at showcase events, over a period of several months. They tried to gather as much data as possible on him from their own in-person scouting observations, from in-home meetings with Seijas and his parents, and from every other source possible.

Still, the team knew it was taking on a financial risk to sign a pitcher, even one with as much potential as Seijas, to such a large bonus because the biggest unknown at that age is whether a player will be able to remain healthy.

It was a gamble Rodriguez and the Cardinals were willing to make.

"It's fun to sign a guy who's already got stuff," Rodriguez said. "He's got some size to fill out, but he's athletic and has a lot of the things scouts look for in a player."

Finding and signing players like Martinez, Reyes, Sierra, Sosa, and Seijas has been Rodriguez's primary job since December 2007, when he was hired by the Cardinals after working as the manager of international operations in the commissioner's office. A native of Puerto Rico, Rodriguez grew up in New York and went to work in the commissioner's office after graduating from the University of Connecticut.

The challenge of his job motivates Rodriguez on a daily basis. One of the biggest questions facing him and others in his same position is how to handle the influx of young Cuban players becoming available.

"As an organization, in general, you have to make a call on if you want to maybe be very aggressive with that Cuban guy who is a little more polished than your typical 16-year-old," Rodriguez said. "You're comparing maybe a 19- to 21-year-old Cuban who has played a lot of baseball and been in a lot of international competition, playing in more organized leagues, versus a 16-year-old kid from the DR who maybe doesn't have as much baseball under his belt and is more about projection. It's an interesting exercise as you go through it."

In preparation for the international signing period, Rodriguez made scouting trips to Mexico, Panama, Colombia, Nicaragua, the Dominican Republic, and Venezuela. He also went to Japan to watch the under-18 world championship tournament.

None of those trips, Rodriguez said, rivaled the most challenging trip he ever took to see a player.

That happened a few years ago, when he was scouting Cheslor Cuthbert, who made it to the majors with the Royals in 2015. Cuthbert lived on Corn Island, about 45 miles off the coast of Nicaragua.

"I remember jumping on a propeller plane being literally two feet away from the pilot and saying, 'What am I doing?'" Rodriguez said. "It was a really old plane. We were going to land and I pretty much had the same view as the pilot.

"I had a home visit and actually had lunch with his parents, then jumped back on the plane to Managua. That was probably one of the more interesting trips I've had. We did have some good fish that day, though."

Despite his efforts, and a good offer, Rodriguez and the Cardinals saw Cuthbert go to the Royals. Dealing with the frustration of not getting a player he really liked is just another element of the job, Rodriguez said.

The personal opinion of the scout about international players is perhaps more important than evaluating players for the amateur draft in the U.S., Rodriguez said, for the obvious reason of not being able to have as much statistical or medical information, and not having as good of a read on the level of the competition a player is facing. In most cases international players are eligible to sign when they are 16, or usually at least two years younger than players in the U.S., who must complete high school.

"Makeup is really important," Rodriguez said. "A lot of the information that is available in the U.S. we just don't have because the kids are so young and the leagues are not as structured.

"Getting into the house, getting to know what makes a player tick, whether he's got competitive drive, that's all a huge part of the equation on my end."

That was the case with the signing of Sierra, an outfielder from the Dominican Republic, and Sosa, a shortstop from Panama, who both signed in the summer of 2012.

"What jumped out at you then was the easy actions in center field, the projectable arm, natural actions in the outfield, didn't have a length to his swing which you always look for in hitters," Rodriguez said about Sierra. "He had no red flags. We haven't had anything but positive things to say about him since we signed him. He takes a million swings in the off-season when he is back in the Dominican."

During his eight years of running the Cardinals' international operations, which included the planning and construction of their new academy in the Dominican which opened in

2015, Rodriguez has seen a lot of changes in how teams operate on the international market, primarily the increase in the amount of money teams are now investing into international operations.

"Everybody is realizing the international market is a place where good talent can be had," Rodriguez said. "Everybody seems to be competing now.

"One change I am seeing is younger and younger players. You go to a showcase and they will say, 'That player is eligible in 2017. He's going to be a stud.' You're looking at 14-year-old kids fielding ground balls and taking BP. Who knows where we are going to be in two or three years?"

And, as soon as they are eligible, those players likely will be signed by the Cardinals or another team. Sierra was 16 when he signed.

From a scouting standpoint, Rodriguez said Sierra likely is further along at this point in his career than he would have expected.

"You really don't know what you are getting at 16," he said. "Some guys take a little longer. He's always had tools but that doesn't always translate into performance. The fortunate part with him to this point is that he has been able to translate those tools into performance."

Sierra spent the 2014 season in the Gulf Coast League, where he led the Cardinals' organization with a .386 average, 30 RBIs, and 13 stolen bases in 52 games. That performance made him the first player from a short-season league to be named the organization's minor-league player of the year.

The Cardinals tried to push the 19-year-old in 2015, jumping him all the way to Class A Peoria to start the season. For the first time probably in his life, Sierra struggled, hitting .191 with 52 strikeouts in 178 at-bats. When the short-season teams began play, Sierra went down to Johnson City, Tennessee, the next level up from the GCL, and hit .315, the top average on the team.

Sosa, also 19, also played at Johnson City in 2015 and showed his potential by hitting .300 while displaying some power potential with seven home runs. That came after he hit .275 in the GCL in 2014.

For both players, their 2014 season in the GCL was their first time playing outside of their native countries, an adjustment which is difficult for a lot of young international players.

"People think rookie ball, Gulf Coast League, it's an easy level," Rodriguez said. "There's a lot of things those players encounter for the first time in getting them settled in the U.S., a new culture, new hotels, things we may take for granted as Americans. You've got to be comfortable with that so you can do your job on the field.

"It's definitely not easy, and you've got to remember pitchers in the Gulf Coast League are not always the best control-wise. When you analyze the entire thing, it was a pretty impressive season."

Rordriguez knows the way he does his job might be changing in the future. There is talk baseball will adopt a worldwide draft in the next Collective Bargaining Agreement, which comes up after the 2016 season, conducting it in much the same manner as the current amateur draft for players from the United States, Canada, and Puerto Rico.

Rodriguez admits he is not certain how he feels about that.

"That's a tricky question," he said. "I'd like to hear more about it. It depends on eligibility. I don't think we're against the draft but so much of it is concepts right now that it's sort of hard to tell."

Until the rules change, however, Rodriguez will be on the go throughout Latin America, hoping for more nights like December 3, 2012, the night the Cardinals signed Alex Reyes.

12   ALEX REYES

SHORTLY AFTER MIDNIGHT, ALEX REYES LEFT THE KANSAS CITY
Royals' academy in Guerra, Dominican Republic, to make the
45-minute drive to the capital city of Santo Domingo, where he
headed to an all-night print shop.

It was the only place he knew that was open and had a fax
machine. Reyes was about to sign a contract to become a professional baseball player, a document that also had to be signed
by his parents in New Jersey and by the team.

As he made the drive, the 18-year-old Reyes did not know
if he would be signing with the Royals, the Astros, or the
Cardinals.

All three organizations had offers on the table as his agent
negotiated back and forth over the phone. Reyes had spent
time over the previous months in each of the three's academies
as they evaluated his potential before he was eligible to sign.
December 3 was the first day he was allowed to sign a contract
by Major League Baseball.

"It was a crazy night," Reyes said.

The Cardinals thought they had a deal completed only to see

it fall apart with some last-minute changes by the agent in the early morning hours.

Moises Rodriguez, the Cardinals' director of international operations, was on a plane heading to Nashville for the start of the winter meetings as he got updates from the team's scouts on the ground in the Dominican.

"I sent Mo (GM John Mozeliak) an e-mail that said we had to convene as soon as I arrived," Rodriguez said. "I told him we needed to get this thing done. We were sweating it out."

Finally about 4:00 AM in the Dominican, the deal was done, the fax machine hummed, and Reyes became a Cardinal.

"When you sign that contract, your job is to play baseball," Reyes said. "It was definitely a life-changing experience. It was a wonderful night. It was an interesting time to see everything happening that you dreamed about. It was a great feeling."

Reyes was finally able to sleep for a few hours before his parents boarded a plane for the Dominican, where the family was reunited to celebrate the contract.

Rodriguez also went to bed happy that night, after the end of a pursuit that had begun with another frantic phone call nine months earlier.

In March of 2012, the Cardinals had their first contact with Reyes, who had made the unusual decision to leave the home where he had been born and raised in New Jersey to move to the Dominican Republic and live with his grandmother.

Reyes had just started his senior year in high school but did not believe he was getting the exposure to scouts that he would get in the Dominican Republic.

"Ever since I was 12 years old I had gone to the Dominican every summer," Reyes said. "I always used to see pro baseball players walking on the street. It opened my eyes. In New Jersey I could say I probably saw one professional baseball player. I thought my chances were better in the Dominican Republic."

It was not a hasty decision. Reyes talked it over with his parents, both of whom work as school security guards. He knew leaving would take him away from his two older brothers and his friends. He would not attend his senior prom or attend graduation with his class.

Reyes made the decision to move.

"They were definitely worried about me," he said of his parents. "I knew I wasn't going to see them for a while. It was tough not seeing my brothers. My parents had been there for me since day one, and it was a tough decision, but at the end of the day I thought it was the best decision for me."

Reyes moved in with his grandmother in San Cristobal, about an hour west of Santo Domingo, in December of 2011. After taking a little time off, he began working out, running on the beach and swimming, and made contact with the local *buscone*, the man who acts as a combination scout, agent, and coach for the local players in the Dominican.

"His name was Juan Baleta, and he kind of took me under his wing and started working with me," Reyes said.

Reyes, then 17, began throwing, and soon, scouts were hearing about this new pitcher in the area. One of those scouts was from the Cardinals.

"I was in a car in Florida driving back from an international event when I got a frantic—in a good way—exciting, emotional phone call from our scouting supervisor saying he had found a pitcher," Rodriguez said. "He told me I needed to go see him as soon as possible.

"When you get that kind of phone call you have to act on it. It wasn't something where I could wait three or four weeks until my next trip. So I went to go see him."

Rodriguez could appreciate the passion of Rodney Jimenez, the area scout who first brought Reyes to his attention.

"He fought hard for Alex after seeing him in Palenque, DR," Rodriguez said. "He brought him to the attention of Angel Ovalles. He felt as strong as anyone about his talent and potential. Rodny's initial evaluation was critical and his involvement throughout the process made the acquisition possible.

"We likely don't sign Alex without Rodney, who sadly passed away in 2014 from heart failure. He will be the proudest person in Heaven if Alex makes the big leagues. He and Ovalles did an outstanding job in helping us land him."

Rodriguez remembers his first trip to watch Reyes.

"He was pretty much as described," Rodriguez said. "He had good size, he was athletic, throwing in the low 90s. His breaking ball needed to be tightened up but it had good rotation and he had a feel for a changeup. He seemed comfortable, and for not having a lot of experience on the mound, he was impressive."

Based on that one workout, the Cardinals made Reyes a low six-figure offer. They knew he wouldn't sign, but making that offer showed the buscone the Cardinals' interest and helped to get his interest as well.

Other scouts were coming to see Reyes and the Astros actually got Reyes into their academy for a while so he could have an extended tryout.

A few months later, Reyes left the Houston academy and the Cardinals picked up their interest as they watched him continue to throw. They made another larger offer, and the buscone agreed to let Reyes go to the Cardinals' academy for a month.

"They wanted to watch me pitch consistently," said Reyes, who was enjoying the process. "I was waiting until I was eligible to sign, but I was having a good time. I was working out and having fun. If you are having fun playing baseball there's nothing you can complain about."

As the months passed, the Cardinals were doing their due diligence and learning more about Reyes, building more of a history with him. "He was becoming more of a priority," Rodriguez said.

The Royals were very interested as well, and had Reyes at their academy as well—up until the night he became eligible to sign.

By this time, Reyes was being represented by Basilio Vizcaino, a well-known agent in the Dominican. After going back and forth, the final decision for Reyes came down to the Royals and Cardinals, and he picked the Cardinals, receiving a $950,000 signing bonus.

"I really liked the Cardinals organization and the way they promote their young guys," he said. "It's all about the home-grown talent, and I saw that as a positive."

Reyes had played more shortstop than he had pitched growing up, but there was no question by then where his professional future was headed.

"Ever since I was a little kid I played with my brothers in the backyard," Reyes said. "I started playing T ball when I was six and my brothers tell me I told our father that I wasn't going to play T ball anymore because it wasn't fun. I was used to my brothers throwing the ball to me. I just always loved baseball. It was always something I wanted to do.

"As I grew bigger and got taller I, got a lot slower running around the bases. I always had a pretty decent arm and always liked to pitch."

The Cardinals sent Reyes to Johnson City, Tennessee, for the 2013 season, and he made a smooth transition to pro ball, going 6–4 in 12 starts with a 3.39 ERA, striking out 68 batters in 58⅓ innings.

Reyes skipped a level in 2014 and pitched the entire season at Class A Peoria, where he made 21 starts, going 7–7 with a 3.62 ERA. He also struck out 137 batters in 109⅓ innings but had some problems with control, walking 61 batters.

Reyes was learning how to pitch, however, and one of the people he was watching closely was a fellow New Jersey native, left-hander Rob Kaminsky, who had been one of the Cardinals' two first-round picks in the 2013 draft.

The two were teammates for all of the 2014 season in Peoria and also spent the first half of the 2015 season together at Class A Palm Beach, before Reyes earned a promotion to Double A Springfield.

"I learn from watching," Reyes said. "I don't think I've ever even told him this or he even knows, but Rob Kaminsky is definitely the number one guy I've studied. From day one in Peoria he just separated himself from everybody on the pitching staff, including me. He was an unbelievable guy. His stuff is good and he knows it's good.

"His focus is, 'I'm going to beat every hitter that steps in the box,' and that's something I kind of just picked up from him without even telling him. I just watched him work and the way he competes on the mound."

Reyes was only 2–5 in 13 starts for Palm Beach, with a 2.26 ERA and 96 strikeouts in 63⅔ innings before he moved up to

Springfield in late July. He had been in Springfield only a few days when he got a reminder about the business of baseball when Kaminsky was traded by the Cardinals to the Indians for major-leaguer Brandon Moss.

"The trade was tough," Reyes said. "I spoke to him that night. It was a weird kind of thing. We had made plans for the off-season to run some camps and things back in New Jersey and I knew it would be different with him wearing a different uniform.

"Baseball is a business, we all understand that. We're human beings and all we can control is what happens on the field."

The promotion to Double A, like the trade of his friend, caught Reyes a little off guard. He had missed a few weeks with a sore shoulder, an injury that cost him a chance to pitch in the Futures Game at the All-Star Game. To get the promotion to Double A one month before his 21st birthday, however, was a nice bonus.

Reyes made eight starts for Springfield, going 3–2 with a 3.12 ERA. The fastball has been Reyes' calling card since his debut, often reaching triple digits. But he knows velocity alone is not going to make him an effective pitcher as he continues his climb through the organization.

The chance to continue to pitch, to learn and improve, was one of the reasons he was excited about his assignment in the Arizona Fall League in the fall of 2015, joining other top prospects from other organizations.

It hasn't taken long for Reyes to shoot up to the top spot in the Cardinals' prospect rankings, but Reyes said he doesn't spend much time—or any—thinking about that.

"I try to ignore it," he said. "You see so many guys in the minor leagues who are great players who aren't ranked as top prospects. I try to just avoid that and have good days on the field and be ready for whatever comes up."

Reyes still has the childhood joy of playing the game, remembering when he had posters of Mark McGwire and Sammy Sosa on his bedroom wall and watched every Yankees game he could on television.

Now, of course, his focus has shifted to the Cardinals. He thinks back to that late night in the print shop in Santo Domingo, deciding on his future, and still believes he made the right choice.

"The people you have around you here are tremendous," Reyes said. "It's why the Cardinals have so much success. It's not so much because of the things they tell you to do on the field, it's because they are all tremendous people, good people at heart who want the best for you."

As Reyes looks back on his decision to leave home, he knows it doesn't come close to being as tough a decision as one of his Springfield teammates had to make just a few months later.

13   ALEDMYS DIAZ

WHEN HE WAS JUST EIGHT YEARS OLD, ALEDMYS DIAZ ALREADY HAD an understanding of just how important baseball is to people in Cuba.

He was playing for the national championship for kids between eight and 10 years old, and the game was broadcast live on television across the country. Diaz hit a home run in the game, and it does not take much prompting for his proud father to pull out a phone 17 years later and find the video on YouTube.

Diaz grew up in Santa Clara. One of the neighborhood children he played with was Jose Fernandez, the 2013 NL Rookie of the Year for the Miami Marlins. Fernandez, two years younger than Diaz, lived on the same block as the Diaz family, three houses away.

"They used to play on the street when they were pretty young," recalls Diaz's father, Rigoberto. "Aledmys never played with a toy. Neither did Jose. They took baseball very seriously. They had a bat and a ball with them all the time."

Diaz was good enough to represent his country in international competitions, traveling to Venezuela, Japan, and Canada.

He also was a good student, especially in math, and considered a career in medicine. One of his high school teachers tried to talk him into giving up baseball so he could become more serious about his academic pursuits.

Diaz knew, however, that there was something special about playing baseball. When he played an occasional game of basketball or volleyball, it was different. That was for fun. He knew baseball was his future.

By the time he was 17, Diaz was playing in the Cuban National Series, the highest level of competition in his country. At age 19 he posted a .294 average, and in the 2011–12 season he raised his average to .315 to go along with 12 home runs in 270 at-bats.

"Unfortunately when you reach that level and are so young, you realize that there is a roof that you can't go past," Diaz said, with his father serving as his interpreter. "You are stuck in the middle and you can't go on."

Diaz was going to college at the same time, and also was a member of the Cuban national team. In the summer of 2012, that team traveled to the Netherlands for an international competition.

Only Diaz knew his life was about to change.

Diaz defected from the Cuban team during that tournament and took up residence in Mexico. The often-difficult journey led him to the Cardinals organization, where he played at Palm Beach and Double A Springfield in 2014 and for most of 2015, before he was promoted to Memphis.

It took about 18 months after Diaz defected before he was finally cleared by Major League Baseball to sign with a team, and he and the Cardinals came to terms on a four-year, $8 million deal.

The elder Diaz's life also changed when he received a telephone call informing him that his son had walked away from the Cuban team.

"We never talked about it," the elder Diaz said. "It was his own decision. I was so surprised he took that step, but everybody has to make his own decision."

At the time Diaz's father was working in Brazil, representing the Cuban government on a project to control malaria in that country. Working in the field of agriculture science had already taken the elder Diaz to Africa for several years. He also taught English and computer science.

Because he had a visa to travel outside of Cuba, Diaz was soon able to join his son in Mexico and has stayed by his side, leaving his wife and a daughter at the family home in Cuba before they were finally allowed to travel to the United States in 2015.

"It was a hard decision but I had to do it," Aledmys Diaz said. "The first fear I felt was to leave my family behind in Cuba. I had a career in Cuba at that point. I had reached the maximum level of baseball there. That was why I made that step."

Any player who defects from Cuba—as dozens have done since Aroldis Chapman in 2009 and others before him—has to go through a process of establishing residency in another country. Even though the United States government reinstated diplomatic relations with Cuba in 2015, the player has to be cleared by Major League Baseball before he can sign a contract.

For Diaz, the process was expected to last about six months, but it became longer and more complicated because of a mixup concerning his birthday, more likely caused by a clerical error than an intentional misrepresentation.

On the baseball documents, Diaz's birthday was listed as January 8, 1990, or abbreviated to 1/8/90. This would have made him 23 in the summer of 2012, and because of his five years of experience in the Cuban National Series, made him eligible to sign a contract and not be affected by signing cap rules on international prospects younger than 23.

Diaz's birthday, however, is actually August 1, 1990, or 8/1/90. Somehow the day and month got reversed, and because of that, MLB ruled that Diaz would not be allowed to sign for a year, a penalty for what was described as lying about his birthday. Diaz's six-month wait in Mexico turned into an 18-month stay in which Diaz was unable to play the game he loved except on a very limited basis.

"Things happen in life," Diaz said. "I think everything happens for a reason. The year helped me mentally. I couldn't play, but I learned that I can't control all of that."

Diaz worked out as much as possible, trying to keep himself in shape. He trained and played with a minor-league team, and often conducted workouts for scouts from various major-league clubs, including the Cardinals.

The Cardinals had been monitoring Diaz ever since he left the Cuban team. Then-scouting director Dan Kantrovitz had actually seen Diaz play in Asia when he was the international scouting director for the A's, and both Matt Slater and Moises Rodriguez of the Cardinals' front office were assigned to keep tabs on Diaz and his situation.

"When we first met with him in Mexico we really liked him and thought there was something about him," Slater said. "As we got to know him more as a person, about his work ethic and his commitment and his team-first type attitude, that drove us more. He has great makeup, he's smart, and he has a great heart. He fit a lot of the things we look for in Cardinals players."

Slater saw Diaz on four occasions, and Rodriguez made multiple visits as well. The Cardinals had seven different scouts file reports on Diaz before he had a final face-to-face meeting with general manager John Mozeliak at a private workout for the Cardinals in Jupiter, Florida.

Mozeliak admitted at the time of the signing the Cardinals were in uncharted territory, but were excited about getting involved in the Cuban market.

"It's always tricky when you think about trying to scout a player who is not currently playing in games," Mozeliak said. "We had to go to a lot of different parts of the world to do this, between having him work out in Jupiter, seeing him in Mexico. We feel pretty confident this is a good fit for this organization."

The Cardinals made a sizeable investment in Diaz, their first foray into signing a Cuban player or a significant international free agent. They knew he had not been able to play for close to two years and that they would have to be patient as he got himself back into game-ready condition.

The Cardinals assigned Diaz to the Double A level, perhaps the toughest level in the minor leagues, where players are often separated between those who will one day play in the majors from those who won't.

For Diaz, the challenge of breaking in at this level was complicated by his baseball inactivity, at least from live competition, and the fact he had not received the same education in the Cardinals' system as his new teammates had received at lower levels.

His first manager, Mike Shildt, was pleased the way Diaz

responded to instruction and saw that he was open-minded and a quick learner.

"He has shown a real ability to adapt and make changes and understand why," Shildt said in 2014. "Every guy in our clubhouse has a rear-view mirror or rookie ball or organizational experiences under their belt and he had to get that on the fly, coupled with him getting his body back in shape and the expectations of a contract that he deserved. He handled it all very well.

"He's respectful and is a quality guy who has been great to work with. He wants to win and he wants to compete and do well. He has a lot of desire. He checks a lot of boxes in how he goes about things in a positive way."

Diaz's biggest problem in Springfield was staying on the field. He was bothered by a sore right shoulder, likely caused by the long period of inactivity before he signed. After starting the year with Springfield, he was forced to miss more than a month from late April through mid-June while he worked to rehab and strengthen the shoulder.

He was on a schedule of splitting time at shortstop as well as serving as a DH before he was sidelined again for another month.

Diaz completed his first pro season with a .273 average and five home runs, but he only was able to play in 47 games, getting 161 at-bats.

"His talent is commiserate with him being here, he's proven that," Shildt said. "His circumstances are a little different, based on how he got here, his journey to get here. He had to leave some family behind and that's a drain. All of the guys who come from different parts of the country or Latin America leave people behind, but they generally know they are going to be able to go back and spend time with them. There is a little more finality with him regarding that. We've talked about that, and he is compartmentalizing it."

Shildt saw glimpses of Diaz's ability—a ball jumping off his bat for a solid line drive, catching a groundball and throwing from the hole to retire a runner at first. Mostly he saw a baseball player, one who is clearly focused on his goal of making it to the major leagues.

"One of the things I appreciate about him is his aggressiveness," Shildt said. "You can't teach the things that he has. You can't teach the way the ball comes off his bat or the way he reacts in the field. It's just a matter of consistency, of playing and learning from his experiences playing.

"Every day is an experience and an opportunity. How you take that opportunity and grow from it is vital to how quickly you develop. Those experiences are not only your own but your teammates', your opposition's. You don't always have to stub your own toe to know that it hurts."

Healthy for the first time, Diaz began the 2015 season playing regularly at shortstop, but still found himself struggling at the plate. He was hitting .235 on the morning of July 8 when he was called into manager Dann Bilardello's office.

The Cardinals needed to open a spot on the 40-man roster to promote first baseman Dan Johnson from Memphis. Because of his performance and the amount of money remaining on his contract, the Cardinals designated Diaz for assignment.

That meant every team in baseball had the chance to claim Diaz, but none did. When he cleared waivers, he was outrighted to Springfield and was back in the lineup two days later.

Something, however, had changed.

Bilardello was not certain Diaz really knew what was happening. Diaz admits he was confused, and called his agent.

"I said, 'What happened?'" Diaz said. "I know it's part of the game. I just want to keep focused on playing every day and doing my best for the team. There was nothing I could do about that."

In reality, however, there was. Whether being rejected by the other 29 teams served as a wakeup call or not for Diaz, nobody will ever know. But starting with his return to the lineup, Diaz began to play better than he had since he signed.

From July 10 through August 22, Diaz posted a .320 average with seven homers and 25 RBIs. That prompted another meeting in Bilardello's office, where this time the manager informed Diaz that he had earned a promotion to Memphis.

Diaz made a smooth adjustment to the higher level, where he was reunited with Shildt, his first manager. In 14 games before the end of the season, Diaz posted a .380 average with three homers in just 50 at-bats.

Diaz believes there was a simple explanation for his sudden success: he was healthy.

"Last year (2014) was the first time I lost game time," Diaz said. "I played for six years in Cuba and played the whole season. I had a really bad first year, but I think it's part of the process. I came into this season wanting to play the full season."

Diaz admits that in retrospect, the injury was only part of the reason for his struggles in 2014.

"Everything was crazy," he said. "I was learning a new language, and it was tough to focus on the field because a lot of things were happening around you. This year I was able to be more focused on the game. You always want to focus on the field, but even as a professional we are all human too.

"I just wanted to work hard. I know it is a process. Even if you work hard it doesn't always mean you get good results. I just want to keep playing."

The way he ended the season convinced the Cardinals to reward Diaz with one of the coveted spots in their contingent assigned to the Arizona Fall League, where every club sends many of their top prospects.

It was a nice reward for Diaz, and shows the Cardinals are still committed to him. He returned the favor by hitting .315 and convincing the team to put him back on its 40-man roster.

Signing Diaz marked a major change in Cardinals philosophy, and if he is successful it will make it easier for the organization to decide to sign more international free agents from emerging markets. Like any decision made for the first time, signing Diaz was a calculated gamble that the team is convinced will pay off.

"He fits the type of players we want to bring in here," Slater said. "He comes from a totally unique circumstance that we've never done before. We've never dipped our feet in these waters, whether it be a Cuban defector or an Asian player, at this level.

"The whole idea in signing him was that he would not have an immediate impact on the major-league club."

A major part of Diaz's development occurred away from the baseball field, adapting to a new country and a new culture. Having his father to share an apartment for the first summer provided him with a calming and steady influence as he made that transition.

One of his Springfield teammates, James Ramsey, since traded to the Cleveland Indians, was impressed by how well Diaz was able to make those adjustments. Having been on mission trips to Brazil and the Dominican Republic, Ramsey had some idea what Diaz had to deal with on a daily basis.

"When you travel there you can be empathetic to just the adjustment phase of living life in America," Ramsey said. "It affects your play as much as the level of the game. You can tell he was raised in a great household, the values that were instilled in him. He understands hard work and he understands everything that he needs to be successful."

As Diaz showed in the final two months of 2015, all of his hard work—and the Cardinals' patience—is beginning to pay off.

"If I keep working at the end of the day the results will be there," Diaz said. "I think I chose the right organization and in the future a lot of things are going to go well for me."

14   MATT SLATER

THE EMERGENCE OF JANG HO KANG AS AN IMPACT PLAYER FOR THE Pittsburgh Pirates in 2015 did not come as a surprise to Matt Slater.

Kang had been a star in Korea for several years before he was "posted" after the 2014 season, opening the way for major-league teams to negotiate with the Korean league to sign him to a contract.

Slater, as part of an enhanced commitment by the Cardinals to scout and consider signing foreign players, had been to Korea to see Kang, a shortstop/third baseman who had hit 40 home runs in 2014 playing for the Nexen Heroes.

In fact, the Cardinals made a sizeable offer to Kang, who ended up going to the Pirates on a four-year, $11 million deal, plus a $5 million posting fee. During the negotiations, the Cardinals did not have any way to predict how many injuries their major-league team would incur in 2015, which prevented them from guaranteeing the amount of playing time to Kang that the Pirates could offer.

"We came up a little short, but that continues to be a possible talent spot for us," said Slater, whose title with the Cardinals is director of player personnel. "We did our work on him. We did have a very competitive post, but it wasn't enough. We did want the player but the Pirates put in more than we did."

The increased commitment by the Cardinals to scout in Japan and Korea, as well as the players who defect from Cuba and other emerging markets around the world, was a logical move by an organization that has proved it knows how to scout amateur players in the U.S. as well as sign talented teenagers throughout the baseball hotbeds of the Dominican Republic, Venezuela, and other Latin American countries.

The rest of the world was an untapped resource, and as more and more players, especially from Cuba, began having success in the major leagues, it seemed like a wise investment for the Cardinals to try to become more active in that market.

Slater refers to it as "the big boy international market."

More players could be on the horizon, which is why Slater spent close to two weeks in the summer of 2015 on a scouting trip to Japan and Korea.

"We really have made a lot of inroads over there the last few years," Slater said. "We are focusing on a few other guys from both Korea and Japan. We are in position to be players on them. There are a ton of Cuban defectors out there, but more and more of them are defecting at a younger age, which makes them capped players.

"There are a lot of 16-17-18-year-old defectors who would be legit first-round picks in the States, but the money to sign them has to come off your international signing cap."

Slater took one trip to the Dominican in 2015 specifically to see a 16-year-old outfielder. He also saw a left-handed pitcher who was 15 when he defected.

"Both of them are first-round-caliber guys, but they just keep getting younger and younger," Slater said.

With the older players who have been playing professionally in their native countries, however, the only restriction is how much money a team is willing to pay. To be an uncapped player, a player must be at least 23 years old and have played at least five years at the highest level in that country.

"If Aledmys Diaz had been a capped player we probably wouldn't have signed him," Slater said. "Our way of operating is to sign quality players and not just go crazy on one player."

Slater's travels in 2015 took him on several trips to Venezuela and the Dominican Republic as well as to Puerto Rico, to Toronto for the Pan Am Games, to Mexico, and to Japan and Korea. He also did work for John Mozeliak on some special assignments before the major-league trading deadline, and also helped out with scouting several players before the June amateur draft.

The primary focus of his job, however, is to decide which international players the Cardinals should pursue, and how far the club should go financially to try to sign them.

"We believe in overturning every rock, but we definitely put a dollar sign on the muscle," Slater said. "When we think the value and the fit is not right, we move on."

On his most recent trip, Slater saw several players he would like to see wearing a Cardinals uniform one day.

"There are two 21-year-old pitchers in Japan who are the top 21-year-old pitchers on the planet right now, in my estimation," he said. "If they came out right now they would be No. 2 starters in MLB right now at the age of 21."

Because of their age, however, and the Japanese rules, neither of those pitchers can be posted for at least two more years.

Another player Slater saw on his trip was a power-hitting first baseman in Korea, Byung-ho Park, who was posted before the 2016 season. Park is 29, two years older than Kang, and even though the Cardinals submitted a bid, Park ended up going to the Minnesota Twins.

Park has spent the last five years with the Nexen Heroes, Kang's old team. Over the last four seasons he has hit 31, 37, 52, and 53 home runs, each year driving in more than 100 runs. For the last three years the right-handed hitter also has had better than a .300 average.

There is a big difference, Slater knows, from scouting professional players in Korea and Japan and watching teenagers from impoverished rural areas in Latin America.

The common denominator is that they are baseball players, and potentially, future Cardinals.

"I've met with players where you walk into their house and they have dirt floors and no glass for windows, just an open space in the wall," Slater said. "The money you are talking about makes the family break down in tears. It kind of puts it all into perspective.

"I tell my own kids all the time that I can't wait until they are old enough to travel with me down there so they can see it—the differences in the living conditions. Every year after Halloween I take my kids' candy down to the Dominican Republic. I have our scout pull over to the side of the baseball field and pass it out to the kids. Just the look on their faces to get American candy is amazing. What is interesting is that the children there, the players, are just as happy. They are not less happy than we are in America. They are running around playing baseball with milk cartons on their hands, but they are happy doing it."

Trying to scout, and evaluate and project, young teenaged players with such basic skills as throwing or hitting a baseball is one of the facets of his job that Slater enjoys the most, an area he is still trying to master even after 25 years in the business.

Slater, who grew up in Fort Wayne, Indiana, was a sophomore at Marquette University, majoring in sports management, when he got the break he needed to get started on a career in the game.

"I was 19 and I knew I wanted to work in sports management but I didn't know if it would be in baseball, basketball, football, or ping-pong," Slater said. "My professor got a call from the Brewers saying they needed some help in their player development and scouting department. I worked for them part-time until my senior year.

"About a month before graduation, the GM, Sal Bando, said, 'We want to put you on full-time as a coordinator in baseball operations and scouting.' I said, 'Sal, that's great, what are you going to pay me?'"

It turned out the offer was not very lucrative, which forced Slater to make a decision. He already had been accepted to law school, which he explained to Bando.

"He looked at me like I was crazy," Slater said. "Like, you would go to law school instead of working in baseball? I ended up taking the job.

"Why was it baseball? Right place at the right time. I never had a dire passion for baseball. I had a dire passion for sports. Once I started working in baseball, that was when my passion really exploded. My desire became learning how to scout players and how to decide which players are the best fit for a team."

Slater eventually left the Brewers for a job with the Orioles, then spent 10 years working for the Dodgers—where he also found time for law school—before being hired by John Mozeliak and the Cardinals in 2007.

He is trying to put all of the knowledge he has gained over the years into his current role with the Cardinals, with the same goal of finding players who he thinks will fit in well with the organization. He is just doing so in other countries.

The international assignments have made for an adjustment in Slater's personal life as well. Now 44, he is married and the father of a 15-year-old boy and 12-year-old twins, a boy and a girl.

"You are a little more disconnected with the family and not as accessible," he said. "If I am at a high school game in rural Nebraska, my wife can still call me, but when I am in Venezuela I have to wait until I get back to the hotel to call. That's the toughest part.

"I think everything I have done has prepared me to have kind of a greater sense of what is important when trying to acquire a player. I pride myself on the fact I can go see a 16-year-old in Venezuela and make an accurate evaluation of his ability and I can also go make an accurate report on Matt Holliday when he was with Oakland and whether we should trade for him or not. Having that calibration is something that aids me greatly in recommending players and putting together a team.

"I've always been passionate about trying to get the right 25 players and not necessarily the best 25—character, makeup guys. It is an emphasis in this organization at all levels. It's something we stress to our scouts. It can be a little harder to determine that with international players because of the cultural differences. Before we signed Carlos Martinez, Dyar Miller and I took him for a walk on the back fields in Jupiter for half an hour talking to him, trying to understand his makeup. It's an important part of the game, on and off the field."

And Slater knows, as does GM John Mozeliak, becoming more active in the international free-agent market is another way for the Cardinals to add talent to the organization.

"Our job is always to be mining for talent," Mozeliak said. "When you are picking 30th in the draft, you don't have the same advantage as if you are picking first, second, third, or fourth. The dollar allotment is tied to where you pick. Internationally, you also have a much smaller pool to work with than if you are finishing last. When you look at how we can fill our pipeline, we are limited through those two traditional models of amateur and international. Looking at other ways to enhance our ability to collect talent was something we had to do."

15   JACOB WILSON

TWO OF THE PLAYERS MATT SLATER SAW AT THE 2015 PAN AM GAMES in Toronto were quite familiar to him, since both already were in the Cardinals' system.

Outfielder Anthony Garcia left the Double A Springfield club to play for his native Puerto Rico, while infielder Jacob Wilson was given permission by the organization to leave the Triple A Memphis Redbirds to join the U.S. team.

Wilson, primarily a third baseman at Memphis in 2015, played second for the U.S. team which won the silver medal, losing the gold-medal game 7–6 in 10 innings to the host Canadians.

Despite wishing for a better outcome in that game, Wilson left knowing he had represented his country, and the Cardinals, well. He posted a .290 average in the eight games with two home runs, four RBIs, and seven runs scored.

"It was an awesome experience," Wilson said. "When you are around new faces sometimes you can learn more. I was with some veteran guys like Casey Kotchman, who has played in the big leagues, and we got to be pretty good friends and I learned a lot from him.

"It was the first time I got to play for Team USA. Gary (LaRocque) called and told me I had been selected, but I really had no clue. I had to look it up on the Internet to see what I was getting myself into. I didn't know what to expect. I just wanted to make sure it was OK with the organization if I went, since it was in the middle of the season. It was really good to go up there and play.

"Playing for your country and not just an organization and trying to bring back a medal was a big deal. The top athletes in the world were there. For some of them, all they do is train year-round for events like the Olympics and things like the Pan Am Games. I shipped a couple of big duffel bags home filled with stuff."

Even before his selection for Team USA, the 2015 season already had been special for Wilson—returning to play in his hometown of Memphis for the first time as a professional—a childhood prediction come true.

Wilson grew up in the Memphis suburb of Bartlett, and when he was in Mrs. Hale's fourth-grade class at Altruria Elementary School, the students had an assignment to write a letter about what they wanted to do when they grew up.

Nine-year-old Jacob wrote that he wanted to be a professional baseball player.

Fifteen years later, Wilson was reminded about that letter when he received an e-mail from that teacher, Michelle Hale, which included a photo of the letter. She had kept it in her files.

"It was pretty cool," he said.

After a good spring training in the major-league camp, Wilson went to Springfield to begin the season. He hit just .225 in his first 34 games, but seven of his hits were home runs, and he had 21 RBIs—which prompted the Cardinals to promote him to Memphis.

Suddenly he found himself back at AutoZone Park, the same stadium where his family had season tickets as he was growing up, where he had gone and cheered for the Redbirds. Former infielder Stubby Clapp was one of his favorite players.

"I was always that kid who sat in the stands and begged the players for autographs," Wilson said. "Now when I see little kids asking for autographs, I have no problem stopping and talking to them and signing for them, because I was that kid at one time. I know how much it meant to me.

"Did I ever know I was going to be here in this position? No. But now that I am it's nice to give back to the community."

There were at least a couple of times along the way when Wilson had a reason to doubt whether he would become a pro baseball player.

Despite success in high school, where he played shortstop, Wilson went undrafted. He also was passed over after his junior season at the University of Memphis, the year most college players are selected.

Fortunately for Wilson, Jay Catalano, the Cardinals' area scout at the time, had taken a liking to him in high school, even bringing him to a pre-draft workout the Cardinals conducted at AutoZone Park.

"I liked his swing," recalled Catalano, now an area scout for the Seattle Mariners. "I think he hit a home run the first game I went to see him, and first impressions always mean a lot. We were interested in trying to make him a catcher. He had a strong arm and good hands. We tried that at the workout. He had never really caught before, and you could tell."

Some teams considered taking Wilson out of high school, but as the draft progressed, Wilson and his family made it known he was going to accept the scholarship to Memphis.

Catalano's responsibilities changed over the next few years, but he again became responsible for the Memphis area when Wilson, now playing third base, was a senior. It was the best season of his college career, ending with a .320 average, a league-high 17 home runs, and Player of the Year honors in Conference USA.

That season, 2012, the Cardinals brought Wilson to St. Louis for a pre-draft workout. Catalano put in a good report and was optimistic the team would select him in the draft.

Those thoughts began to change in the draft room, however, as the Cardinals used three of their first six picks on third basemen—Stephen Piscotty, Patrick Wisdom, and Carson Kelly.

"You always say you take the best player available, but you've got to have a place for him to play," Catalano said. "As the rounds ticked by I could see what was happening, that he was being bypassed because we had too many third basemen.

"About the fifth or sixth round I texted him and asked if he could play second base. He texted back and said, 'I never have but sure I can do it.' I told Dan Kantrovitz (then the scouting director) that he could play second. He said, 'Really?' and I said, 'Sure.' He stayed there a few rounds longer than we had expected, and Dan finally pulled the trigger in the 10th round."

As a college senior, Wilson had no bargaining leverage and signed for $20,000 and headed to short-season Batavia to play second base.

"I got to know his family," Catalano said. "He's a really nice kid but not too nice, if that makes sense. He has a hard-nosed attitude at the same time. He was one of those guys that you know when he gets out in the minor-league system, the player development staff is going to like him, and that's always helpful to get more opportunities.

"He is one of those guys who just seems like he keeps getting better."

One of the ways Wilson did that was to play the game the only way he knew how—with a desire to work hard, to learn as much as he can from those around him and never take anything for granted.

"I feel like one thing I've been pretty good with is keeping my emotions under control," Wilson said. "I've always been kind of mellow with everything I did. It's still baseball. I just go out and play and let things happen the way they are going to happen; that's the only way to really go about it. If you do that, things usually will work out for the best."

It helped Wilson, of course, to be playing at home during the 2015 season.

"It's fun to go out and play and know there are a lot of familiar faces in the stands and to know that people are coming out to watch you," he said. "It adds an extra level of excitement to the game."

While Wilson did not hit for as high an average as he would have liked in his first Triple A season—hitting .231—he did show some power, hitting 11 home runs and driving in 56 runs in 89 games.

Adding in the seven home runs he hit in Springfield, Wilson finished the year with 18—which led all players in the Cardinals' farm system.

"It (hitting home runs) started to come to me in my senior year in college," Wilson said. "I was trying to make sure I drove the ball. I've taken that same approach ever since then. It's one part of my game that I try to maintain."

Wilson, who also hit 18 home runs in 2013 before a knee injury cut his 2014 season short, knows there are not a lot of "traditional" power hitters in the Cardinals' system.

"We don't have to hit a lot of home runs to win games," he said. "We are able to produce good hitters who can still have good power numbers, getting hits with runners in scoring position, hitting a lot of doubles, things like that."

Even in his brief career, Wilson has had an opportunity to mix with players from other organizations. He played two years in the Arizona Fall League, adding to his Pan Am experience, giving him a chance to compare notes.

"A lot of people say, 'One day we want to play with the Cardinals to see what it's like. We hear about 'the Cardinal way' and all these good things and we don't get to experience it face to face," Wilson said. "I think the biggest difference about the organization to me is how much they care about their players and how much they are willing to push them and give them opportunities. I'm not sure other organizations do that.

"You are held to a higher standard here. The organization is not going to deal with trouble on or off the field. That helps produce a lot of good guys. This room is filled with great teammates with great personalities who at the same time are guys who find ways to win games.

"It's not always about having the best players, but about having guys who can play together as a team. This organization finds the right guys who fit into that clubhouse. You are taught that coming up through the minors and held to that standard.

"There's a way to look out for your own career and still be

a good teammate, whether that's a little thing like sacrificing yourself to get a guy over late in a game or hitting the ball to the right side. That shows you care about winning but also about finding a way to help the team. You can't just go out and play for yourself. You have to take care of your own business but help find a way to help the team at the same time."

Putting the team first also comes into play when the organization asks a player to change positions, as the Cardinals did in 2015 with Rowan Wick.

16   ROWAN WICK

ROWAN WICK HAD A FEELING THAT SOMETHING WAS GOING ON when he was called into Palm Beach manager Oliver Marmol's office.

"I had been playing once out of every three days for about two weeks," Wick said. "I knew something was up, but I can't really say I saw it coming."

"It" was what Gary LaRocque, the Cardinals' director of player development, had to say when Wick came into the office and closed the door.

Despite the fact Wick had been one of the few power hitters in the Cardinals' farm system, setting a team record for home runs at State College, Pennsylvania, in 2014, LaRocque was delivering the message that Wick's days as an outfielder were over.

The team was moving him to the mound.

It's something the Cardinals have done with other minor-league players in the past, with good results. Jason Motte was about to be released as a catcher when he began pitching in 2006 and five years later he was closing out a World Series. Sam Tuivailala had spent two years in rookie ball as a light-hitting shortstop before he started pitching in 2012, and barely two years later was on the mound at Busch Stadium.

The 22-year-old Wick was going to be the next convert.

Wick was one of only four players in the Cardinals' minor-league system who hit 20 or more home runs in 2014; Randal Grichuk hit 25, Xavier Scruggs 21, and Wick and Mason Katz both finished the year with 20. Fourteen of Wick's home runs came in 35 games and 119 at-bats at State College, breaking the franchise record.

That performance earned Wick a promotion to Class A Peoria, where he hit his last six home runs of the year, but posted only a .220 average.

When Wick's offensive struggles continued at the start of the 2015 season—hitting just .198 with 50 strikeouts in 126 at-bats with only three home runs—LaRocque decided it was time to make the change.

"He said he didn't see my bat playing any higher so it was time to try the next best thing, pitching," Wick said. "At first I wasn't very happy about it because of how the 2014 season went, and the year before that I had a pretty solid year. I thought I was kind of coming along as a hitter.

"Obviously 2015 wasn't great for me; there are a lot of good pitchers in high A and I was seeing pitchers who consistently were throwing off-speed pitches for strikes. I guess I just couldn't handle it, so he decided to make the switch."

Wick already had changed positions once before. He was a catcher when the Cardinals scouted him at Cypress Community College in California, making him their ninth-round pick in 2012. He caught that summer for the GCL Cardinals before moving to the outfield the following year.

Wick was all in favor of that move, believing it would allow him to concentrate more on the offensive part of his game.

He admits it is going to take a little longer to get used to the latest switch, and it didn't help that his first summer as a pitcher was spent mostly in the training room and sitting and watching others pitch.

Wick's first summer as a pitcher consisted of three games covering a total of two innings, back at the GCL level. He allowed four hits and walked two, which produced two runs, while striking out one.

He told the trainers that his elbow felt a little sore, so they shut him down for about 10 days, then started him on a rehab program—and Wick never got back on the mound.

"I don't know why," he said. "They didn't push me at all. I could have had a few opportunities to pitch. I was ready to go for about three weeks. I wasn't too happy about that."

Wick already had some concerns about how to adapt to the schedule for pitchers, which is far different than that of a position player who is in the lineup every day.

"Pitching is 100 percent boring," Wick said. "The bottom line is pitching is boring. You stand around and shag in batting practice for an hour. When you're playing the outfield you shag but you use that time to focus on getting your reads and work on your footwork. Then you get to hit and you focus on your swing. Then you work on your baserunning. Batting practice is when you do your work.

"As a pitcher, you just stand there and catch the balls that come to you."

Wick knows that if he does have some success on the mound it will no doubt improve his attitude about changing positions, but it's also easy to understand why Wick feels the way he does.

"I thought they would give me a full season to try to figure it (hitting) out," Wick said. "Maybe I would have hit in the second half. My childhood dream was to hit in the big leagues. Now I'm trying to get there as a pitcher."

Wick had those dreams when he was growing up in North Vancouver, British Columbia. He also played hockey, rugby, and soccer. His father was a rugby player in Canada but it was baseball that was special to Wick.

When he was 15 he was asked to play for Team Canada. He hit two home runs on the Canadian junior national team that finished fourth in the world championships in 2010. Even though he also had spent a little time on the mound in youth baseball, like most young players, Wick was focused on hitting even then.

And that was never more true than in the summer of 2014.

Assigned to State College to begin the short-league season, Wick hit two home runs on opening day, June 13. He repeated that performance three days later.

He had 10 home runs before the month was over, and by the time he was promoted to Peoria on July 22, Wick's 14 home runs established a franchise record. It was not the first time Wick had gotten hot at the plate. In Johnson City in 2013, he hit five of his 10 home runs in an eight-game span.

When you are on that kind of roll, Wick said, it is fun to come to the ballpark.

It was harder when he found himself back in the Gulf Coast League, where games are played under the summer Florida sun on back fields with no scoreboards and few fans. Motivation is

Davis Ward was the last pick in the final round of the 2014 draft, but that hasn't stopped the Cardinals from giving him every chance to make it to the big leagues. (Davis Ward)

The Cardinals were scouting another player when Arturo Reyes caught the eye of scout Matt Swanson. (Mark Harrell/ Springfield Cardinals)

Jordan Swagerty has learned to appreciate every pitch he throws after spending almost three seasons on the disabled list. (Mark Harrell/Springfield Cardinals)

Ben Yokley thought his baseball career was over after graduating from the Air Force Academy in 2015 before he received a phone call from Cardinals scout Aaron Krawiec. (Johnson City Cardinals)

Oscar Mercado, the Cardinals' second-round pick in 2013 out of a high school in Tampa, Florida, became the first player in the minor-league organization to reach 50 steals since 2004, in 2015. (Allison Rhoades/Peoria Chiefs)

Dealing with adversity was a new experience for Jack Flaherty in 2015 after finishing his last two years of high school with a record of 23–0. (Allison Rhoades/Peoria Chiefs)

Austin Gomber posted a 15–3 record with a 2.67 ERA in 22 starts with Class A Peoria in 2015, leading the Chiefs to their first playoff berth in five years (before they became a Cardinals affiliate). (Allison Rhoades/Peoria Chiefs)

Blake McKnight was born and raised a Cardinals fan in the St. Louis suburbs; the team selected him in the 38th round of the 2013 draft. (Allison Rhoades/Peoria Chiefs)

Xavier Scruggs has played nearly 900 games in the Cardinals' minor-league system, making stops on five different teams, spending most of the 2014 and 2015 seasons at Triple A Memphis. (Roger Cotton/ Memphis Redbirds)

Despite not having played catcher since the eighth grade, Carson Kelly moved from third base to behind the plate in 2014. (Brian Walton/ TheCardinalNation.com)

Oliver Marmol was a 23-year-old infielder in 2010 when he was released by the Palm Beach Cardinals. In 2015, he took over the team as its manager. (Christopher Shannon/ State College Spikes)

Steve Turco has been managing in the rookie league for 13 years, learning the value of patience along the way. (Brian Walton/TheCardinalNation.com)

Travis Tartamella has been instrumental in developing pitchers throughout the Cardinals organization. In 2015, he made his major-league debut at the age of 27. (Mark Harrell/Springfield Cardinals)

harder to find, and Wick admits he has had to work at that, a task that was even harder when he was not even able to pitch.

He is hoping to learn to use his hitter's mentality to help him think like a pitcher.

"I've never really watched pitchers before," he said. "I've never focused on mechanics. 'What pitch was he throwing?' I've never thought about mound presence. It's changed how I even watch big-league games. I'm paying attention to how they don't slow down their arm on off-speed pitches or don't tip their pitches. There is a lot more to it than you think.

"(The move) was definitely emotional. I'm still not over it, to be honest with you. I want to hit. I want to hit in batting practice."

One of the people who is watching how Wick progresses as a pitcher, and rooting for him, is Tuivailala. He remembers the day he was given the same message a few years ago—that if he was going to have a future in the organization, it was going to be as a pitcher.

"That was always Plan B going into my professional career," said Tuivailala, who had much more pitching experience in high school than Wick before the Cardinals drafted him in the third round in 2010 out of a California high school. "They wanted to see me as a position player first. Obviously we all have a clock on us and they approached me and said they were thinking about putting me back on the bump. They said, 'We think it's going to help out your career and possibly let you move faster.' I was all for it. I was just happy they thought to give me another chance."

What made it easier for Tuivailala than Wick was his past pitching experience and the fact that he had not had the offensive success that Wick had in his first couple of years in the minor leagues.

Wick's move came at a time when the Cardinals were struggling to find power hitters in their system. They did not have anybody in their farm system in 2015 who hit more than 18 home runs. The entire State College roster, where Wick hit 14 home runs by himself the year before, hit 19 in more than 2,500 combined at-bats.

Most baseball instructors believe hitting for power is one of the last tools to come for a player, which is why the Cardinals do not put a high emphasis on home runs in the system, especially at the lower levels. They did draft a couple of potential power hitters in the 2014 and 2015 draft, high schoolers Justin Bellinger and Kep Brown, but each elected to go to college instead of sign with the Cardinals.

"The very first thing we focus on and work on with players who have raw power is learning their strike zone," LaRocque said. "We expect and hope that once they gain the number of at-bats they need, that you start to see that power translate into game power. One tends to lead to the other.

"We want them to develop into good hitters, guys who can hit for average as well. The combination is very important. We don't expect to see high numbers (of home runs) because we don't put a premium on it. They are still developing as pure hitters."

And if that development should stall, the organization always can make them a pitcher.

"I feel like they've got a good eye about who they want to switch things up with," Tuivailala said. "They know when somebody has the potential to switch. It was definitely a blessing for me to get another chance. It's worked out pretty well.

"When they first brought up the transition, they brought up Motte's name. They talked about his success. It was good to hear that. I was all for it. From that day forward I forgot I was a position player and just worked on pitching."

That's exactly what Wick is trying to do. If he can match the success of Motte and Tuivailala, maybe he will become more accepting of the change. Like both of those pitchers, Wick projects as a reliever, where he could rely mainly on throwing fastballs in the mid 90s.

"I've always had a plus arm," Wick said. "I know they are going to be patient with me and give me some time to figure it out. If it works out, hopefully I will pitch in the big leagues. That's the idea, right?"

Wick's goal of pitching in the majors is no different than every other pitcher in the system, even those who are a long way from St. Louis or didn't even throw a pitch during the 2015 season, like Davis Ward.

17   DAVIS WARD

THE SMALL GROUP GATHERS EVERY MORNING INSIDE THE TRAINING
room at the Cardinals' facility in Jupiter, Florida, members of
their own team.

There were no games for this team during the 2015 season,
just physical therapy sessions followed by workouts designed
to keep them in shape as they go through the months of rehab
that follow Tommy John surgery.

It has become by far the most common surgical procedure
in baseball, especially among pitchers, and for most of 2015, at
least four pitchers in the Cardinals organization were in various
stages of recovery following their operations.

"We call it Club Rehab," said Davis Ward, who had his surgery on May 7. "One guy is about six months ahead of me, and
another is about two weeks behind me. Everybody is at different stages, but it is really helpful to talk through everything that
is going on. There is camaraderie on a team, there is camaraderie in extended spring training, and there is camaraderie in rehab.

"It's good to have that cross-section of guys in different
stages of rehab to bounce ideas off on. It's a good resource."

Ward, a 23-year-old right-hander, found out he needed the surgery in April after trying to rehab an ACL strain suffered when he was pitching in his first pro season in the Gulf Coast League in 2014.

"It was a minor enough strain that I didn't need surgery, so I tried to rehab it, but then I came to spring training and was in the extended program and it started hurting more," he said. "They decided it was bad enough that it needed surgery.

"I would rather go ahead and fix it than keep trying to rehab it, even though it was frustrating because I had never had any arm problems before."

So for the first time since probably seventh grade, Ward did not play baseball in the summer. Pitchers going through Tommy John rehab are on a set schedule; after several weeks in Florida following the surgery, they are allowed to return home for several weeks, mainly to allow the elbow to heal, before reporting back to Jupiter.

For most pitchers, it will be 12 to 14 months from the date of the surgery before they can be back on the mound pitching in games.

"It's kind of a bizarre little world," Ward said. "All my buddies in the organization were still playing, so you try to keep up with them the best you can, but if you are not in the clubhouse every day you're out of the loop. You miss all the stories that get told in the clubhouse. You miss that camaraderie.

"I've never not thrown for six to eight months since I was a really small kid. Once you get home and get in a rhythm you get more comfortable but you definitely miss the game."

For Ward, home meant time spent back in Little Rock, Arkansas, where he tried to make the most of his free time by relaxing with family, taking weekend float trips with friends, or visiting friends that he never would have been able to do while playing.

He also used the opportunity to get his wisdom teeth pulled, electing to do all four at the same time.

The one thing he didn't do was spend any time worrying about what will happen when he does get back on the mound and tries to throw again.

"I think one of the things that people mention but don't really talk enough about with Tommy John surgery is the mental aspect of it," Ward said. "You know it's going to be a year and a lot of times the psychological part of it can wear you down and be tougher than the physical aspect of it. You don't play for so long and you really aren't doing much and you can't tell if you are getting any better.

"I know for a lot of guys in my situation, being a late-round pick, when you go through a tough injury guys worry that if they do get back, how long is their career going to last? My goal is to throw again and get back on the mound and pitch and just enjoy the game. I'm not worried about the end game. Essentially I feel like I am playing with house money. I love this game and every day I'm playing it is a blessing."

Ward has that attitude because he wasn't just a late-round pick, nor was he just a *last*-round pick (the 40th round in the 2014 draft)—he was the *last* pick in the *last* round, the 1,215th player selected, following his senior year at Ouachita Baptist University, an NCAA Division II school of 1,500 students in Arkadelphia, Arkansas.

The NFL has made a big event out of being the last pick in that sport's draft, giving the player a title, Mr. Irrelevant, and making him the guest of honor at a week-long celebration in Newport Beach, California, that includes a golf tournament and a banquet, complete with a trophy presentation.

When Ward hung up the phone after getting the word he had been drafted by the Cardinals, he celebrated by going out to dinner with his father at one of his favorite spots in Little Rock, a sushi restaurant.

"I thought Mr. Irrelevant was for both sports, but I found out it was just for football," Ward said.

The knowledge that there would be no special celebration of his status did not disappoint Ward. He had what he really wanted—an opportunity. He received the standard $1,000 signing bonus and reported to Jupiter.

"He deserves a chance," said Dirk Kinney, the Cardinals' area scout who recommended Ward. "He's been highly successful, he's got a really good cutter, he throws strikes, and he's going to make people beat him."

The Cardinals, more so than many organizations, have shown in recent years that they can find quality prospects at small colleges. It's a perfect blend of trusting their area scouts, such as Kinney, and the team's quantitative analysts, who have come up with a system to take players from small schools and determine how they compare to players from larger, more well-known schools.

Of the 84 players selected by the Cardinals in the 2014 and 2015 drafts, 31 were from small four-year colleges or junior colleges.

"Our quantitative analysis guys were very impressed with him," Kinney said of Ward. "They play a big role in this. We've got really good guys there, and they have a really good relationship with the scouts."

There have been times in the past when the statistics of a player from a small school have been so dominant that the analytics department, or "baseball development" as it is called by the Cardinals, recommends that an area scout go see that player. Other times it is the scout who brings up a player, then looks to the analysts to verify and support his opinion.

"You need to see these kids," Kinney said. "You want to give them a shot and see what they can do. With guys from small schools, the cross-checkers usually never get to see them. It gives the area scouts a sense of pride to get one of these kids because it means the organization is showing trust in you."

In Ward's case, what Kinney saw in person and the analysts confirmed was an ability to throw strikes with multiple pitches. The 6-foot Ward was a two-time conference pitcher of the year, and for his junior and senior seasons combined, was 20–8 with 17 complete games. In 214⅓ innings, he struck out 167 batters and walked just 34.

As a senior, Ward was 10–5 with a 2.60 ERA after going 10–3 with a 1.74 ERA as a junior. He also was awarded a Division II Gold Glove as a senior. He tied the school record for career wins, ranks first in career complete games, and is second all-time in strikeouts.

"Control is something that has always come pretty naturally to me," said Ward, who also was named the best college player from Arkansas playing in the state as a junior and senior. "I can throw six pitches, and I can work backward in any count and throw any pitch at any count. I change speeds pretty well and I can locate my fastball, changeup, and cutter. I like missing barrels and getting outs."

Kinney had a relationship with Ward that pre-dated the 2014 draft. Kinney spent two seasons as an assistant coach at

Ouachita Baptist, followed by time as an assistant at Arkansas–Little Rock before switching to scouting. He had recruited Ward out of high school.

Ward's older brother, Dustin, a left-hander, was drafted in the 19th round by the Orioles out of Central Arkansas in 2011 and spent two seasons in Baltimore's system before he was released.

Coming out of high school, Ward had offers from bigger colleges in Arkansas, such as Central Arkansas and Arkansas State, but chose Ouachita for its combination of academics and baseball. He earned his degree in business marketing.

"The advice from my high school coach was to choose a school that was the best fit regardless of baseball," Ward said. "I knew I would love to play baseball at the next level, but I knew it might not happen, so I wanted to have a good career to fall back on and that's why I chose Ouachita."

What pleased Ward the most as he began his pro career was that he quickly learned he had the ability to compete at the next level.

It was a small sample size, just five games covering 16 innings, but Ward posted a 1.69 ERA, struck out 10, and did not walk a batter during his stint in the GCL in 2014.

"The biggest thing to me in the transition was, as far as I could tell, there was not a jump in competition," Ward said. "I thought I would get hit harder but I got confidence that I can get outs. The biggest thing I had to get used to was the amount of Spanish spoken in the locker room by all of the Latin American players. That was a culture shock to me."

Another fact that Ward had to deal with was the reality of being paid to play baseball, but that didn't turn out quite as well as he had hoped.

"I ran a deficit for the summer, and I think that's pretty common," he said. "Almost everybody has to get an off-season job. I did some landscaping and some computer work for my uncle. I think last year after expenses for every two weeks I cleared about $100.

"It was one of those things where you dream about playing baseball, and it's a perfect time for me because I don't have a wife or kids. So making minimum wage is fine for me. It's not much but you get to play baseball."

Thinking about playing again is one of the ways pitchers like Ward, and the others on the Club Rehab team, can get through the monotony of the process.

The group has frequent discussions celebrating the small highs and battling through the inevitable lows. Cory Jones pitched in just five games in 2014 before his surgery. Blake Higgins is recovering from his second Tommy John surgery. Ward also has watched Tyler Melling, Steven Gallardo, and Keith Butler go through it before him. Fernando Baez had his surgery about two weeks after Ward's operation.

"It's easier to manage when you break up the timetable," Ward said. "You think in smaller increments—'I'm going to be playing catch in three weeks, and in three more weeks I will be throwing 90 or 120 feet.' That makes it much more manageable."

It is not uncommon, however, for Ward to wonder about what will happen when he does get in a game again.

"The main thing I am worried about is how it's going to feel at the start," he said. "I'm a touch pitcher, with a cutter and sinker, and I rely on command. That's my strong suit. And they say that is usually the last thing to come back. It's going to be hard to get a lot of polish on my pitches."

As he enjoyed spending hot summer days on a raft floating down the Buffalo River, being back on the mound seemed a long ways off for Ward.

"It does cross your mind, especially with an elbow injury," he said. "I had been cleared to do a lot of stuff, but I was worried about…what if I fell off and hit a rock or something, a freak accident?"

When he does get back, one thing Ward knows is that his own performance will dictate the next steps in his career.

"When I was drafted and got into the program I was told, 'We don't look at Baseball America rankings or 'top prospects,'" Ward said. "It's a merit based system. That's what they preach, and for the most part that's true. If I do well, hopefully I will move up."

That was exactly what happened in 2015 to the player selected by the Cardinals in the last round in the previous draft, pitcher Arturo Reyes.

18   ARTURO REYES

MUCH AS THEY HAD WITH THE SELECTION OF MICHAEL WACHA WITH their top pick in the 2012 draft, it was very early in the 2013 college baseball season when the Cardinals zeroed in on left-handed pitcher Marco Gonzales as their targeted first-round pick.

Matt Swanson was the area scout in the northwest part of the U.S. at the time, so naturally he spent a good deal of time that spring watching Gonzales at Gonzaga University in Spokane, Washington.

A funny thing happened that spring, however. While Swanson was there watching Gonzales, he found another pitcher on the Gonzaga staff that he liked as well—a right-hander named Arturo Reyes.

"It was kind of interesting how it worked out," said Swanson, now the Cardinals' cross-checker for the Midwest region. "It was funny they turned out to be the bookends of our draft. Marco was more of a known commodity but Arturo has really taken off once he got into pro ball."

The Cardinals used the 19th overall pick to draft Gonzales and, after making 39 other selections, took Reyes with their

40th-round and final pick. By then, 1,186 players had heard their names called by one of the 30 major-league teams.

"I really didn't have any contact with the Cardinals until the day of the draft," Reyes said. "But I know they saw me come in behind Marco and close out some games. I also started some games, and I am sure that had a little to do with my selection."

It was not automatic even after the draft that Reyes would sign with the Cardinals, because he had other options. As a junior, he could return for his senior season, perhaps assume more of a leading role on the pitching staff in the absence of Gonzales and improve his draft stock.

He also was set to spend the summer of 2013 pitching in the prestigious Cape Cod League, the home of some of the top college players in the country, and a good performance there would have no doubt brought him more attention as well.

But Reyes was intrigued by the Cardinals. The question he most wanted answered was the same one Davis Ward and other late-round picks before him had or would ask: would his draft status affect his opportunity to prove he belonged?

"That was a big question I asked," he said. "I wanted to know when I went to spring training if I was going to have that number on my back. Was I going to be treated like a 40th-round draft pick? Or was I going to be the same as everyone who is there fighting for a spot?"

Swanson understood the question and was ready with his answer.

"I think we do a better job than any organization I know of once you sign, you are going to get an opportunity," Swanson said. "We have had many kids who have thrived as an under-valued pick. Every year or two it seems we have a guy or two, and it's exciting to get those types of guys. As scouts you look up years later and say, 'That was an amazing pick.'"

Reyes hopes that is his story as well, and that there will come a day in the not too distant future when he is not described as the "other" Reyes, top pitching prospect Alex Reyes, or the "other" pitcher from Gonzaga, besides Gonzales.

"I talk with (scout) Braden Looper all the time about how he found Trevor Rosenthal, and with Brian Hopkins about signing Matt Adams," Swanson said. "It's such a combination of scouting and player development, but ultimately it falls on the player. You do have a little lesser of an opportunity than if you are a higher pick, but so many of these guys don't care and they just go out and do their job and pass by guys who were taken a lot earlier in the draft and got a lot more money.

"Every single year I think we beat the other 29 teams on small-college guys. A lot of teams live and die by the 80 and 20 rule, meaning 80 percent of their picks come from bigger schools. At the end of the day, it's hard to argue with our track record."

Assured that he would get the same opportunity as other pitchers, Reyes signed and was sent to State College, Pennsylvania, and all he has done in the three years since is keep pitching well and earn a promotion, reaching Triple A Memphis in 2015.

"We could have taken him 30-something rounds earlier and looked pretty good," Swanson said. "You really take pride in guys like him. At the end of the day there was still a reason why he was a 40th-rounder. He's a little undersized, but he is really athletic, with a really good delivery and a really good mix of pitches.

"I think he fits the mold of what we look for, especially in pitching. It's tough to go out on a limb for a 5-foot-11 or 6-foot right-hander but you could tell there were a lot of things that you thought would take in pro ball. We have a track record of taking guys and molding them into something special.

"I would be lying if I said what he is now is what I thought he would be, but it's exciting for me and a good reminder that scouting isn't static. You can look up in a couple of years and see that you were wrong about a player, but in the right way."

Reyes admits that the challenge of proving he deserved to go higher in the draft was one of his biggest motivations to succeed.

"My goal is to learn something new every day," he said. "We have a little more room for failure in the minor leagues than in the majors, and that's where we all get most of our life lessons, through failure. What I appreciate about the game is learning from those failures. A lot of people deal with it or get beat up by it, but I try to see the advantages of what I can take out of it."

Reyes has used his friendship with Gonzales from their one year together at Gonzaga as a resource, but much of his advice and counsel has come from his other brother, Jorge, who was a 17th-round pick by the San Diego Padres in the 2009 draft out of Oregon State and has pitched in the Padres and Braves organizations since then.

"As a kid you see games on TV but you don't think of everything that goes on outside of the game itself," Reyes said. "I kind of had a little idea because of my brother, and that way I kind of came in knowing a little bit of what to expect. It's still amazing to me to see all of the work that goes on behind the scenes."

Sometimes the easier part of the job, Reyes knows, is actually pitching in games.

"The mental preparation is so important," he said. "It's easy if you have a good game because you can sit on that for a couple of days, but if you have a bad game you're not going back out there for another five days, so you have to sit on that. Sometimes it can be pretty hard.

"Dealing with some of the failures and success is the biggest thing I have learned so far. You can't be too satisfied with a good outing and you can't be too down after a bad game. There has to be a new approach every time you go out there."

In his short career, Reyes has had a lot more good games than bad ones, starting with his first season in State College, when he posted a 2.08 ERA splitting time between starting and pitching in relief.

He started 22 times for Class A Peoria in 2014, making one relief appearance, and went 6–8 with a 3.67 ERA. He struck out 104 batters and walked only 34 in 122⅔ innings.

Reyes made just three starts at Class A Palm Beach in 2015 before he was promoted to Double A Springfield, where he was 7–7 with a 2.64 ERA in 17 starts before he finished the season at Memphis, making five starts.

"I've been real excited about the way things have gone here, and how I've been treated," Reyes said.

Reyes also understands, however, that baseball is still primarily a business and sometimes an organization has to make tough decisions. He saw it happen with Jordan Swagerty.

19   JORDAN SWAGERTY

FOR MORE THAN THREE SEASONS, JORDAN SWAGERTY SPENT MORE
time on the disabled list than he did on the mound.

One of the conclusions he reached somewhere along the way
was that he really appreciates the game of baseball, something
he admits he had always taken for granted in the past.

It wasn't until Swagerty spent all of 2012, most of 2013, all
of 2014, and the early part of the 2015 season unable to throw
a baseball that he realized how much the game meant to him.

Which was why, when he finally got back on the mound for
Double A Springfield in 2015, he vowed to make the most out
of every pitch, every inning, every game.

"I have an appreciation for every out I get," Swagerty said. "I
used to go out there and throw and go home and not think about it
anymore. Now every time I get an out I know what I did to get it."

When Swagerty walked off the mound after his final appearance of the 2011 season, his first year as a professional after being selected by the Cardinals in the second round of the 2010
draft from Arizona State, he had a right to feel proud of his
accomplishments.

He had risen to Double A in just five months, advancing
through three levels of the organization, and was ranked that

winter as the Cardinals' 10th-best prospect by Baseball America. He finished the year with a 1.83 ERA for the first 36 games of his career.

Swagerty had no way of knowing then that over the next 43 months, he would spend more time than he ever would have imagined possible in a training room or a doctor's office, unable to pitch. Most of his time was spent doing the lonely task of rehabbing his right elbow after three separate surgical procedures, including Tommy John surgery.

The only games he was able to pitch during that span came in a one-month stretch from June to July in 2013, a total of nine appearances covering 10 innings split between the Gulf Coast League Cardinals and the Class A Palm Beach Cardinals. He knew things weren't right, and his career went back on hold.

Hurdles is the word Swagerty uses to describe that challenging ordeal.

"It was tough," he said. "It's one of those things that makes you a stronger person. Going through it taught me a lot of life lessons. No matter how things turn out for the rest of my career, I know I overcame something and took steps in the right direction as a person with my character and other aspects of my life."

The first sign that Swagerty was having elbow problems came in spring training in 2012. Surgery followed in April, knocking him out for the season. The issue in 2013 was a pinched nerve on the outside of his elbow which required more surgery, and in 2014 he had to undergo another cleanup to have a bone spur removed.

"I could dissect an elbow," Swagerty said of all the medical knowledge he has gained because of his experiences.

"It's hard with Tommy John not to go nuts at first because there is so much you can't do," he said. "I love to go to the gym and shoot baskets, or play golf, and I love to hunt, but you can't do any of that. I did learn how to do some things left-handed. I learned to play the guitar a little bit."

He also watched baseball, and learned more about the game he thought he already knew from having played it since he was a young boy growing up in Texas.

"Doing a lot of the rehab at the complex in Jupiter, I really was never far away from baseball," Swagerty said. "I watched a few games in extended spring, and went to some of the Palm Beach games at night. I was still there, I was still learning, I was just not on the mound.

"I found myself paying more attention to the game. I learned from the things that were going on. During that time I wouldn't have thought it would help me when I got back out there, but I will say now that it played a big part. I know I am still learning and growing.

"It's funny. I was away from the game a long time, but my sense on the mound is a really calm feeling. It feels like I've played all of those years with the knowledge and experience I gained."

Swagerty found himself back in Springfield on May 7, 2015, making his season debut with a scoreless inning against Northwest Arkansas. He knew he was not 100 percent, but being able to pitch at all was a major victory.

"You see the flashes, it comes and goes, a pitch here or there and you go, 'Wow,'" said Springfield manager Dann Bilardello. "When any athlete comes off an injury the main thing for them is to feel like they are healthy. You have to get over that hump, whatever it is, like a football player with a knee injury."

Swagerty pitched in 20 games for Springfield and could not get over struggles with his control, experiencing more poor games than good appearances. Ultimately, in July, the Cardinals made a decision to release him.

It was a reminder that not every story in baseball has a happy ending.

Swagerty had prepared himself for that possible outcome. If it had to happen, he was at least glad it happened after he was able to spend a couple months back on the mound instead of getting released when he was not playing.

"I appreciate every part of the game," he said shortly before he was released. "Every time I go out there I know it could be the last time I throw. Anytime you have multiple surgeries there is no guarantee that it's going to last forever. It's something I don't take for granted anymore. I really try to go out there and enjoy every moment.

"Before the injury you think you can play forever. Afterward, you appreciate the fans. When you are away from the game for a long time, you appreciate the parts of the game that you never did before."

That is a piece of knowledge that Swagerty, who turned 26 a couple of days after he was released, wanted to pass along to his younger teammates. He looks at them, especially when he was around those just beginning their careers, and sees himself.

"It's definitely a way for me to talk to younger guys," Swagerty said. "I've been through a lot and most of the guys can understand and respect that. They listen. It's a way for me to help, especially with guys just coming from the draft. Hopefully they can take away a couple of things from me, and learn to appreciate the game and play hard every day like it could be your last."

Swagerty acknowledges that he might not have the attitude he does now without the help, encouragement, and support of his family. His father, Presley, is a successful businessman, author, and motivational speaker, and his sister, SaraBeth, is a rising country singer in Nashville.

"My dad is a real positive guy," Swagerty said. "Having somebody like that as a role model, and my mother as well, has helped me. There were plenty of days when I felt down and I sent them a text or called them and got nothing but positive words in return—'Keep your head up, keep pushing, this is something you will get through.' When you have people driving you to be better every day, even when you are down, that's what keeps you going."

Swagerty admitted that being separated from the game for three years changed him more off the field—and those changes will last the rest of his life.

"I'm a better person," he said. "I have patience. I used to not be a very patient person. The way I view life has changed. Whenever you view it as 'I'm a baseball player and it's never going away'; I don't know if that's the best way of looking at life.

"When it's kind of taken away from you a little bit, it changes your character. It builds your character. When I came back and was playing, I appreciated the game 100 times more. That's a big step forward."

Another player who appreciated the chance he got to pitch in the Cardinals system in 2015 was Ben Yokley, who knows he won't get that chance again for at least two more years.

20   BEN YOKLEY

WHEN BEN YOKLEY WALKED OFF THE MOUND FOR THE FINAL TIME as a student at the Air Force Academy on the morning of May 22, 2015, he thought his baseball career was probably over.

Then he got a phone call from Aaron Krawiec.

Krawiec covers several western states as an area scout for the Cardinals and paid attention to Yokley during his four years at the Academy, even though the schedule had not worked out for him to see Yokley pitch in a game during his senior season.

With just a couple of weeks to go before the June draft, Krawiec wanted to see Yokley throw one more time, so the two arranged for Yokley to throw a private bullpen the evening of May 28.

That day happened to coincide with the Academy's graduation ceremony.

"I tossed the hat in the air, then went back over to the baseball field and threw a bullpen and long-toss session," Yokley said. "It was about 30 pitches total; that was it."

Krawiec saw what he needed to see to recommend the Cardinals use one of their third-day picks on Yokley, who set a career record with 95 appearances for the Falcons and came armed with a mid-90s fastball.

"I kind of kept it on the down-low," Krawiec said about his interest in Yokley. "I didn't know how many other guys knew about him or what their perception of the situation was."

Krawiec knew that drafting a player from the Air Force Academy was different than selecting a senior from almost every other college or university. It meant dealing with a military commitment, and the reality that the team would have to wait to get the full benefit of having the player in the organization.

It also, however, had other benefits which were appealing to Krawiec, and also to Chris Correa, the Cardinals' scouting director at the time.

"You are always looking for high value wherever you can with seniors," Krawiec said. "Ben is an athletic kid and has a really good arm and hopefully it will work out.

"I know how hard it is to go through those service academies and what type of person it takes to make it through that. I won't say that made my mind up for me—because you still need the tools from a baseball sense—but he has the makeup and the right mindset."

It didn't hurt that right-handed reliever Mitch Harris, from the Naval Academy, had paid dividends for the Cardinals in the recent past. Harris had to serve nearly five years of active duty in the Navy before beginning his baseball career, and made it to the majors after a little more than two minor-league seasons.

"I had a feeling the experience that we had with Mitch and how that has turned out wouldn't hurt the situation," Krawiec said. "When I turned in the final reports and talked to Chris, he was all for it."

Even though Harris' story had been well documented, Yokley, a native of Arvada, Colorado, said he was not aware of it until he got a text message from his mother after she heard about Harris making his major-league debut.

"She said the Cardinals just had a pitcher make his debut from the Naval Academy," Yokley said. "I looked into his story a little bit and saw he was on the exact same track I am on now. I haven't gotten to talk to him about it, but it definitely makes me hopeful."

Yokley was in the gym, working out, at the Academy when he got another phone call from Krawiec on the morning of June 10, informing him the Cardinals were going to take him with one of their upcoming picks. They did, choosing him in the 29th round.

Yokley was only the seventh player ever selected in the major-league draft from the Air Force Academy and the first pitcher. None of the first six reached the major leagues.

He had largely given up hope of being drafted after he was contacted by the Tampa Bay Rays during his junior season but went undrafted. He talked to the Rays again briefly, he said, at the start of his senior season but then had no more contact with them or any other team until the phone call from Krawiec.

"They (scouts) don't even look at us here, so I just said I was going to go out and pitch my senior season and play while I still could," Yokley said.

It was a solid season. In 27 games, Yokley was 2–0 with four saves for a team that went 23–29. He recorded 45 strikeouts in 34 innings.

Following graduation, each of the newly commissioned Second Lieutenants receive two months of leave before reporting to their first assignment. Yokley had planned to spend most of the break in Colorado, working to obtain his private pilot's license, and traveling to several weddings of friends.

It turned out that Yokley had to alter those plans. He packed up in mid-June and headed off to Johnson City, Tennessee, to see what the low levels of professional baseball were all about.

The biggest change between college and professional baseball, Yokley found, was being able to concentrate 100 percent on baseball for the first time in his life.

"It was kind of nice going to the field with a clear mind," he said. "When you go to the field, they trust that you know what you are doing and what you were drafted to do and know what your job is."

For Yokley, that job was the same one he had with the Falcons—coming out of the bullpen throwing strikes. He made seven appearances for the rookie-level Cardinals, working a total of 13⅓ innings. He recorded 15 strikeouts with only four walks, and had a somewhat inflated ERA of 5.40 because of a couple of multi-run games.

In one of those games, on July 20 at Bluefield, Yokley did something he never did during his four years pitching at Air Force—he gave up two home runs. Yokley had faced 593 batters in his college career without ever allowing a home run.

"It was more similar to college than I was expecting," Yokley said of his conversion to the professional ranks. "Most of the guys in the league were either guys directly from college like me or a couple of years out of high school. There was a similar approach from hitters for the most part, and from the pitching side, we were doing what they taught in college—trying to get low strikes. The hitters here seem to have more power and more speed."

The biggest lesson Yokley took away from the six weeks in Johnson City was that he could compete as a professional, but he knows he is going to have to wait until he can resume his career.

"It would be a different story if I got absolutely shelled, if you throw your best and it gets hit," Yokley said. "But I saw you can make a mistake or two and still have success. It definitely was a positive experience because you know you can be better than this and you are still having some success. It was encouraging to see that happen."

Said Krawiec, "I think he did a good job, coming from where he was, getting his feet wet in professional baseball. I think it was a good step in the right direction."

Yokley reported back to the Academy in Colorado Springs on July 28, where he was assigned to work in the athletic department, specifically in an administration position with the baseball team, until he was scheduled to begin pilot training in April 2016 at Vance Air Force Base in Oklahoma.

A business management major, the 23-year-old Yokley is excited about this next phase of his life as well.

He knows he will not be allowed to play baseball for the Cardinals again for at least two years. Because of his work with the Academy's baseball team, however, he had the opportunity to continue throwing and keep his arm in shape much more easily than did Harris, who had to get his throwing in wherever possible, often on the deck of a ship.

"I won't start pilot training until next April and they can't let me have all that time off," Yokley said. "So they are letting me go back to the Academy. I am going to be helping with recruiting and will work as an assistant pitching coach and teach a PE class until my training begins."

After two years, if he so desires, Yokley will have an opportunity to apply to have his five-year active-duty commitment reduced to two years because of his status as a professional athlete. The Air Force does not have to grant that request, which also would then require Yokley to serve six years in the Reserves instead of three. He would be allowed to play baseball during that period, however.

Yokley knew about that commitment when he made the decision to go to the Air Force Academy out of high school, a decision he knows was the right choice for him.

"I wasn't looked at by many Division I colleges," Yokley said. "There were a couple here and there with decent scholarships but were not very competitive programs. That was the first indicator to me that I should go get a good degree, because you don't want to be at a school just for baseball.

"I knew it was going to be pretty hard for four years, but I knew it was what I needed to do. It was definitely a challenge. There were days when you said, 'I'm done with this, I'm so fed up, I want to get my life on track and do what I want to be doing.'"

Two years from now, Yokley hopes that involves once again playing baseball in the Cardinals organization.

"Hopefully, we will be able to work that out," Yokley said.

Another player who was excited about his future after the 2015 season, for a different reason, was Oscar Mercado.

21 OSCAR MERCADO

season, someone said that a particular minor-leaguer ran well, with plus speed, but "can't steal a base."

"Somebody spoke up and said, 'How do we know? He only had a handful of attempts?'" said field coordinator Mark DeJohn.

That conversation led to the development of a plan to identify certain players and try to give them 70 stolen-base attempts over the course of a season.

"The idea was that at the end of the year, we would have a better evaluation," DeJohn said. "The analytical guys also were involved and determined that stolen bases do not really become a positive factor unless you are successful 73 to 74 percent of the time."

The three players specifically identified by the Cardinals all had the type of season the organization hoped for, led by Peoria shortstop Oscar Mercado.

Mercado, the Cardinals' second-round pick in 2013 out of a high school in Tampa, Florida, became the first player in the minor-league organization to reach 50 steals since Papo Bolivar stole 51 in 2004 for Double A Tennessee.

His 50 steals, in 69 attempts (a 72-percent success rate) led the Class A Midwest League, making him one of two league leaders in stolen bases in 2015. Outfielder Charlie Tilson stole 46 (out of 65 attempts, a 71 percent success rate) to lead the Double A Texas League.

The third player the Cardinals hoped would run more was Palm Beach outfielder C.J. McElroy, who finished the season with 39 steals out of 55 attempts. He ranked third in the Class A Florida State League.

The caught-stealing totals can be a little deceiving because they often include runners being picked off base.

In 2014, Mercado led the short-season Appalachian League with 26 steals, out of 33 attempts; Tilson was 12-of-22 between Palm Beach and Springfield; McElroy was 41-of-59 at Peoria.

"It was a point of emphasis, we encouraged it, to get him to run a little more," Peoria manager Joe Kruzel said of Mercado's attempts. "Oscar is fearless when it comes to trying to steal a base. He'll attempt to steal second and third. It's one of his strengths.

"Like anything in this game, part of a player's development is to try to develop his strengths."

Mercado, who played all of the 2015 season at the age of 20, was a couple of years below the average age for the Midwest League. He was happy with his success—but knows he can get better.

It was his first full season as a professional, playing 117 games, and he achieved his stolen-base totals with a .254 batting average and a .297 on-base percentage, drawing only 23 walks in more than 500 plate appearances.

"It's been a learning experience," Mercado said. "In high school you can get away with bad jumps if you're fast; the catchers aren't as good. Out here you have to be focused and dialed in all the time. If you don't have a good jump you have to dial it down."

DeJohn said it has been his experience with many young players that even if they have enough speed to steal bases, they are often afraid to run for fear of being thrown out.

"If you give kids the green light they won't go, so you have to make them go," DeJohn said. "Then they feel like, 'You gave it to me, it's on you.' Until you get them to the stage where they say, 'I know I can do this,' they will make an excuse because they are afraid of being thrown out. It's hard to convince guys, but it's just like a pitcher developing a pitch.

"A guy in Johnson City might be throwing 94-mph and striking guys out, and his attitude is, 'Why would I want to develop my slider?' He is just trying to compete and get through the inning. You've got to convince kids that you don't care if they give up a run because they threw a couple of sliders, even though you hope they don't. They need to throw the slider on the first pitch because they don't want to throw it later if they are behind in the count.

"It's harder than you think—that number goes under their name. And in the end, we use those numbers to try to evaluate them."

Mercado is an exception to DeJohn's theory, because he often had the green light and wasn't afraid to run. He knows his speed is going to be one of the factors that will determine his advancement through the organization.

"It's definitely a big part of my game," he said. "As soon as I get on I look at Skip and see what signs he is giving me. He kind of lets me be on my own. I've learned a lot, how you have to pick and choose your spots. I'm trying to get better.

"I'm not afraid to run. If the situation is right you just kind of have to go. You're only going to get better at it if you run. If you are scared to do it you're not going to be successful."

Coming out of high school, Mercado was considered a likely first-round pick but slid into the second round. He had the option of accepting a scholarship to Florida State, but instead signed with the Cardinals.

At the time there was a definite shortage of shortstop prospects in the organization, but with Mercado's success, the improvement of Aledmys Diaz in 2015, and the play of Edmundo Sosa at Johnson City and league MVP Allen Cordoba of the GCL Cardinals, that no longer seems to be the case.

In Mercado's case, one of the areas where he hopes to improve is on defense, where his speed can sometimes be a detriment, letting him get to many balls that other shortstops might not reach. Many of his 41 errors came on errant throws.

"Errors are going to be there, and you have to learn from them," Mercado said. "I'm going to become better at it. You have to try to stay aggressive and not let the errors get to you. If you do that, you're just going to make even more. You have to keep your head up, because you know the next one is coming to you."

Said Kruzel, "He played a demanding position. He gets to a lot of balls because of his range. Sometimes the official scorer gave him an error that I didn't think he deserved."

Before he was drafted, Mercado had heard a lot about life in the minor leagues. Still, he never anticipated a couple of the incidents that occurred to his teams in 2014 and 2015.

The most bizarre happened in Johnson City in 2014. After a game in Greenville, Tennessee, on July 11, the team's bus driver quit, literally taking the keys to the bus and walking away, leaving the team stranded.

"He said we can find our own way home," said infielder Chris Rivera.

Mercado said he and the other players found out later the driver was frustrated because he thought the team was taking too long to get ready to leave for the trip back to Johnson City following the game.

"What's worse than losing?" Mercado asked that night on Twitter. "Losing, and then the bus driver quitting and taking off with the bus keys."

It took about four hours before the bus company was able to get a bus to pick up the team and make the 30-mile drive back to Johnson City.

"I didn't understand the situation," Mercado said. "At the time all we could do was laugh. There was no point in getting angry."

After a game in Cedar Rapids, Iowa, on May 14, 2015, Mercado and his Peoria teammates boarded the team bus for the three-hour trip back home about 9:40 PM. Near Iowa City, however, the bus blew a tire.

That started an all-night adventure that didn't end until the team finally made it back to Peoria about 5:30 AM, about five hours behind schedule.

Two of Mercado's teammates, outfielder Blake Drake and pitcher Matt Pearce, also had been present for the Johnson City episode.

"We've had some eventful trips," Mercado said. "It's not the minor leagues if you don't have those moments."

Mercado can only hope, however, that those moments become fewer and further between as he advances through the Cardinals' organization.

"I know I have a ton of room for improvement. As I get older and move it's going to get better," he said. "I want to learn from everyone around me and become the best player I can be."

Pitcher Jack Flaherty, one of Mercado's teammates in 2015, shares the same goal.

22   JACK FLAHERTY

ONE OF THE LESSONS YOUNG PITCHERS HAVE TO LEARN IN THE MINOR leagues is how to deal with adversity.

For Jack Flaherty in 2015, that was virtually a brand-new experience.

Going 23–0 as a high school junior and senior did not offer Flaherty many opportunities to learn how to cope with failure. He pitched a no-hitter in his final game and was named the California high school player of the year by Gatorade.

"It just showed that in any decision, I didn't get a loss," he said. "It's not like I got a decision every time I went out. I gave up runs, I got hit, but the team was able to put up runs every time I pitched and I was able to keep the game tied or win the game.

"As a pitcher all I try to do is put my team in position to win the game. I've tried to carry that over into pro ball."

Flaherty was the Cardinals' second pick in the 2014 draft after his glittering prep career at Harvard-Westlake High School in Los Angeles. He was the 34th overall choice in the draft, the pick the Cardinals received as compensation for free agent Carlos Beltran signing with the Yankees.

The Cardinals gave him a \$2 million signing bonus to get him to turn pro and give up a scholarship to the University of North Carolina.

With that bonus came high expectations, but Flaherty didn't worry about that.

"I have the highest expectations for myself, higher than anybody else," he said. "I expect the most out of myself."

Flaherty also is realistic, however, and knew that at age 19, pitching in the Class A Midwest League for the Peoria Chiefs was going to be a lot more difficult than pitching in high school. If he didn't already know that on his own, he found out with a couple of quick phone calls to friends.

Two of Flaherty's former teammates in high school were both first-round selections in the 2012 draft after their senior years at Harvard-Westlake. Left-hander Max Fried was the seventh overall pick, by the San Diego Padres, and the Washington Nationals selected right-hander Lucas Giolito with the 16th overall pick.

"I've talked to both of them about the baseball side of things and the lifestyle side of the game," he said. "I feel like I was more prepared on the lifestyle side about what to expect as far as the bus rides, the hotels. There's stuff you have to deal with, but in the end you are doing what you want to do, which is go out and play baseball every day."

And, Flaherty has learned, some of those days are a lot rougher than others. Those lessons started on Opening Day, when Flaherty was the Chiefs' starting pitcher on April 9 against Quad Cities.

The Cardinals, as they do with virtually all of their prep pitching prospects, had brought Flaherty along slowly during his first summer as a professional in 2014. He made only eight appearances, six of them starts, and pitched a total of 22⅔ innings for the rookie-level Gulf Coast League Cardinals. He was 1–1 in those games with a 1.59 ERA, giving up a total of four earned runs while striking out 28 and issuing only four walks.

As the Cardinals had done with some other young prospects in the past, they jumped Flaherty all the way to Peoria to start the 2015 season, basically skipping two levels, and then named him the Opening Day starter.

Flaherty lasted just three innings, giving up only one run, but threw 54 pitches before he had to leave the game because of discomfort in his right shoulder.

It was another aspect of the game he had never had to deal with before.

"Things just didn't feel right when I was on the mound," he said. "I couldn't really tell what it was, but it just didn't feel normal. We had kind of a long half inning and everything just tightened up when I went out and tried to throw. I just didn't think I would be benefitting the team to try to throw without feeling comfortable and I didn't think it would benefit myself either."

The Chiefs took Flaherty out of the game as a precautionary move, and sent him back to Florida to rehab his shoulder. He didn't come back until the end of May but then stayed in the rotation for the rest of the season.

Flaherty posted a 9–3 record with a 2.84 ERA for the season in 18 starts. Only three times did he give up more than three runs, but that was three times more than Flaherty would have liked.

On August 24, pitching at Cedar Rapids, Flaherty failed to get out of the first inning, allowing six hits and a walk which produced five runs, while recording only one out.

There were a lot of lessons for Flaherty to learn that night.

"I definitely think failure is something you have to deal with," he said. "It's not always going to be a smooth ride. You have to be able to work through and try not to be discouraged.

"With rough outings, there is always a learning curve. There's always something to learn. Maybe it was just one of those days but there is always something you can take out of the game, how you deal with it, how you show yourself on the mound."

That game came after a stretch in which Flaherty went 8–0 in 13 starts, impressing manager Joe Kruzel.

"For him to pitch through some of the stuff he's pitched through and to put himself in the position he's in, you have to tip your hat to the kid," Kruzel said. "He's really come along in a short period of time. He's got real good command with good deception and movement on his fastball. He's got a good breaking ball and his changeup is developing.

"He throws three pitches for strikes in any count, and for a 19-year-old kid to be able to do that every six days, we're really pleased. The biggest thing that stands out is his command. He started out this season probably pitching at the league level but by the end of the year he was above the level of the league. It's been a positive year for him."

Flaherty agrees, and has been able to enjoy his success while taking his occasional lumps and realizing how new he is to pitching.

Flaherty was also a third baseman in high school, expecting to play both positions at North Carolina, and has only really focused on pitching for about four years.

"My mom has pictures from our apartment when I was like three or four of me holding a bat watching a baseball game," he said. "She took me to games when I really young. This is just what I always pictured myself doing. It's kind of a dream start-ing to come true.

"I really didn't start focusing on pitching until late in my sophomore year in high school and the start of my junior year. This is the first time I've just been straight pitching and haven't had to focus on other aspects of the game. I can really work on my craft, learning the ins and outs of it."

And Flaherty knows that to get where he wants to get, he will have to keep making progress and keep improving.

"You have to make more adjustments," he said. "I have to control the zone better and throw my off-speed pitches for strikes. I have to try to be able to read hitters more. I didn't call my game in high school, the coaches did, and now I work with the catcher to see what we want to do with each guy.

"I have to keep improving all my pitches. I have to be more consistent and repeat my pitches and my delivery. That's the big thing. You see guys in the big leagues and that's what they do. It all will come with experience."

And part of that experience comes from talking to his former high school teammates. Their conversations, Flaherty said, in-clude his friends questioning him about the Cardinals.

"They want to know how we do things," Flaherty said. "That's something everybody wants to know. I try not to share too much, but I give them what I can. They are my friends so I want to be as honest with them as I can without trying to give any secrets away.

"They are just trying to get better; the same thing we are all doing. I want my friends to succeed."

One of Flaherty's friends, and Peoria teammates, Austin Gomber, certainly found success in 2015.

23 AUSTIN GOMBER

WHEN THE CARDINALS REPORTED TO SPRING TRAINING IN 2013, they had one left-handed starter on the 40-man roster: Jaime Garcia, who had spent a good portion of the previous season on the disabled list.

They had two left-handed starters in camp as non-roster invitees, John Gast and Tyler Lyons, and that was reflective of the entire organization, which had a definite lack of left-handed starters.

It was not a coincidence that the team's top two picks in the amateur draft four months later were both left-handed starters—Marco Gonzales and Rob Kaminsky. The team also used its fifth- and sixth-round picks on left-handed pitchers, Ian McKinney and Jimmy Reed.

The Cardinals used three more picks on southpaws through the eighth round of the 2014 and 2015 drafts, one of whom was Austin Gomber, picked in the fourth round in 2014 from Florida Atlantic University.

Gomber got off to a solid start as a professional, going 2–2 with a 2.30 ERA in 11 starts in 2014 for short-season State

College, Pennsylvania, enjoying the thrill of winning the New York–Penn League championship.

The 21-year-old really broke into the ranks of the organization's top prospects, however, with his accomplishments in Class A Peoria in 2015.

The 6-foot-5 Gomber posted a 15–3 record with a 2.67 ERA in 22 starts. In 135 innings, he allowed just 97 hits, walked 34, and struck out 140. He led the Midwest League in wins and strikeouts and helped lead the Chiefs to their first playoff berth in five years (before they became a Cardinals affiliate).

He believes his success has been a result of the adjustments he made as he moved from college baseball into the professional game, quickly realizing that a good mental approach is just as important as physical talent.

"The first year they had pretty strict pitch counts and innings limits, and that was a little different," he said. "I didn't have the opportunity to go out there every five days and go seven innings. I felt like when I got to Peoria they took the leash off a little bit. Not having the inning limits and pitch counts has been fun.

"I came into this year with a goal of having a good year and putting myself in a position to have a chance to move up, and I think I did that."

Gomber's season actually got off to a slow start as he won only one of his first four starts—but then he got on a roll that didn't stop until the season was over.

In 18 starts from May 5 through August 29, Gomber went 14–0 with a 2.24 ERA. He won all four of his starts in August, allowing just one earned run in 25 ⅔ innings.

"The game is a little quicker, the hitters are better, and the game changes a little bit," he said. "I'm becoming more mature, understanding the game more. You know there are going to be ups and downs, and you try to deal with them as they come, and just go out there every time with a clear head and try to give your team a chance to win."

Only twice did he allow more than three earned runs in a start in that four-month stretch, and he still ended up winning both of those games.

It didn't take long for Gomber to realize that being drafted by the Cardinals would turn out to be one of the best days of his life, even if his pro career got off to a rather unusual start.

He and new teammate Collin Radack met at O'Hare Airport in Chicago when they were on their way to State College, but got stranded overnight when their flight was canceled and they could not find a hotel room.

"It was an interesting day and an interesting night," Gomber said, "but it was all good."

It also didn't take long for Gomber to begin learning what was special about the Cardinals organization, a level of expectation, on and off the field, that he believes is not the same in other places.

"The way we do things is a little bit different," he said. "Everything we do here is very structured. We always wear the same thing; we have a dress code, on the field and coming to the park. We can't wear hair down to our neck or have full beards. I think we just present ourselves in the right way, and that carries over all the way to the big leagues.

"You just are expected to represent the organization well. It's much bigger than the Peoria Chiefs or Austin Gomber. The St. Louis Cardinals have a particular image, and we are just trying to uphold that image. The way we do things here is second to none and we take pride in what we do, we take pride in putting these colors on every day. It doesn't take long to get into the routine of what you are supposed to do and how you are supposed to carry yourself, on and off the field.

"You have to take care of business between the lines, and that's something we are proud of. Everybody knows what is expected of them and we don't have much trouble with that."

Gomber didn't have much trouble on the field either in 2015, which he hopes is a trend that continues as he climbs through the organization.

"At this level you are just trying to get to the next level," he said. "Everybody hopes that one day you will be able to help the club in St. Louis, but that's a long way from here. To get to that point you have to do everything right, and that's something we try to do every day."

After growing up and playing college baseball in Florida, Gomber's knowledge of the Cardinals has increased dramatically since he joined the organization.

For one of his teammates in 2015, that knowledge came at a much younger age.

24   BLAKE McKNIGHT

UNLIKE MANY PLAYERS IN THE ORGANIZATION, INCLUDING JACK
Flaherty and Austin Gomber, Blake McKnight already had a pretty
good knowledge of the Cardinals even before he was drafted.

That's what happens when you are born and raised in the St.
Louis area and are a baseball fan; the Cardinals are part of your
DNA.

"Other guys maybe grew up cheering for other organiza-
tions that maybe haven't had as much success," McKnight said.
"To me this is just what we do; we go to the playoffs every year.
It's just a matter of how far we are going to go."

A right-handed pitcher, McKnight was born and grew up in
the St. Louis suburb of O'Fallon and was a frequent visitor to
Busch Stadium. When he wasn't there or playing the game himself, he was watching games on television.

His favorite Cardinals moment is easy to recall.

"Albert Pujols hitting the home run off Brad Lidge of the
Astros in the playoffs," McKnight said. "I was watching at home
and I remember going nuts. My dad was upstairs and I remember yelling at him."

McKnight was 14 at the time, and of course had no idea that he would become a part of his favorite organization just a few years later. Unlike many of his teammates, McKnight really wasn't even thinking about a career in baseball as he went through school and prepared for college.

McKnight's odds of becoming a professional baseball player likely would have been impossible to measure at that time, considering in part that he didn't even play the sport on a high school team; he and his four brothers and sisters were homeschooled.

McKnight's father, Tom, helped organize a team for youths who could not play on a traditional high school team and that team even won a national championship, with Blake winning MVP honors. He also was able to play on an American Legion team.

That experience convinced McKnight that he wanted to play baseball in college, but there was one obstacle in his way.

"I wasn't recruited by even a single college," McKnight said. "I basically went to Evangel (a small NAIA school in Springfield, Missouri) and had a private tryout and ended up getting a little money on a JV scholarship. I consider myself a walk-on since I went to them and wasn't recruited by anybody.

"I was playing shortstop and pitching on the JV team and four years later I ended up being the first guy ever drafted from the school. When you think about it, it is kind of amazing."

Area scout Dirk Kinney found McKnight and convinced the Cardinals to select him in the 38th round of the 2013 draft, the 1,145th player selected. McKnight had gone from throwing about 80 miles per hour when he was a freshman to hitting the low 90s just four years later.

Kinney had driven from his home in Kansas City to Springfield during a snowstorm in January of 2013 to attend a showcase, where he saw McKnight throw at an event that was mostly for high school seniors.

"Driving down there I thought maybe I should turn around," Kinney said. "But I continued on, and man, it worked out well. I'm thankful it snowed, looking back on it, because a lot of (other scouts) weren't there."

Kinney tracked McKnight's progress throughout the season, watching as he needed just 73 pitches to throw a seven-inning shutout in one game and winning the Heart of America conference championship game 2–1, allowing just three hits.

"You have to give him a pat on the back for working his tail off," Kinney said. "Have I ever come across a small-school kid whose velocity jumped 12 miles per hour over four years? No.

"His plus stuff is what gets you drafted, but all of the other stuff is really important. His makeup is just awesome. He's an awesome kid. His stuff warranted him getting a chance to play professional baseball."

And McKnight has certainly made the most of that opportunity in his first three years in the organization, reaching high A Palm Beach in the 2015 season.

"I've had the chance to talk to some seniors in high school about going on to play college baseball and I think back to when I was a senior in high school," McKnight said. "I've given pitching lessons the last couple of years, working with kids from high school down to about eight years old, which is really young, and I think back to when I was that age, not knowing what I was doing. I loved baseball but I was not maximizing my talents.

McKnight took a realistic approach to his success, and had the same attitude whether he had a good game or pitched poorly.

"I just wanted to go out and pitch and find out what would happen," McKnight said of his pro debut in Johnson City, Tennessee, in 2013. "After my first outing I said, 'I can be successful at this level.' I moved to Peoria and had some ups and downs, but there were periods when I threw the ball well, too. Then in 2015 I was promoted to Palm Beach and had the same approach.

"I try to be honest with myself and the pitches I throw. Maybe I had a good game, but I always think about what I need to do to be successful at a higher level. Does my slider need to be better? I probably got away with some pitches over the plate that I won't get away with at the next level. That to me is about the only time I look at the next level. What do I need to be better at up there?"

McKnight started 10 of his 11 games at Johnson City, going 3–1 with a 2.69 ERA. He split time between starting and relieving in Peoria in 2014, and was in the bullpen again for the start of the 2015 season, where he posted a 1.71 ERA before he was sent to Palm Beach.

After making five relief appearances, McKnight found himself starting again as the team moved another pitcher out of the rotation to try to limit his innings total. McKnight made six starts before the end of the season, including flirting with a no-hitter against Jupiter on August 18.

McKnight did not allow a hit or walk through the first six innings, with the only runner reaching base when he was hit by a pitch. McKnight lost the no-hit bid with two outs in the seventh.

"It was exciting. It was unfortunate it had to end," he said. "Their two hits weren't very well hit, they just found a spot.

That's baseball right there. I've never thrown a no-hitter. I had a one-hitter over seven innings in a game in Peoria, and in college once I had a perfect game going but got taken out of the game because the plan going into the game was that I was only going to throw a certain number of innings."

McKnight doesn't know if the Cardinals project him as a starter or a reliever going into 2016, but he plans to be ready to do either—trying to repeat the success he had in 2015, which he believes started with the work he put into getting better during the off-season.

"I had a better idea about how to prepare," McKnight said. "I was able to get into Rams Park to long toss and I had a better schedule. The first off-season I was in Springfield trying to throw outdoors in 40-degree weather. Things weren't as planned out because they could change because of the weather.

"Honestly, I think most of your progress is made during the off-season. You can work on stuff during the season, but what you do with those couple of months in the off-season is huge."

Giving lessons to younger players in those months actually has proved helpful for McKnight's own development, he said.

"I have an iPad with an app that breaks down the slow-motion video," McKnight said. "Breaking down mechanics gives them an opportunity to see what they are doing, and it helps me understand what I believe about pitching. I see what they are doing and I also can look at what I've done wrong. It gives me a better understanding of the mechanics at the same time I am helping them."

McKnght hopes to pick up a little more velocity on his fastball and also wants to improve his secondary pitches, knowing that will be a key to his continued rise through the organization.

One thing McKnight, like other low or undrafted players, has found to be true is that once a player is in the Cardinals system, where that player came from really has no bearing on his chances for success.

"They really stress that where you were drafted is not going to affect how you move in the organization," he said. "I haven't felt that somebody else got preference over me because I was a 38th-round pick. They treat almost everybody the same. Naturally the top guys are going to get a little more attention because they have a lot of money invested in those guys."

McKnight has seen others rise from very long odds to reach the majors, and that gives him encouragement as well. He also is motivated to be one of the few players from the St. Louis area to play for the major-league team. David Freese did it, as did Kyle McClellan.

During his first pro season in 2013, McKnight was one of four players from the St. Louis area on the Johnson City Cardinals. Two years later, he was the only one of the four left in the organization.

In addition to McKnight, other St. Louis–area players in the organization in 2015 were pitcher Kyle Grana, who led Peoria with 24 saves; first baseman Luke Voit, who hit 11 homers for Palm Beach; relief pitcher Sasha Kuebel, who was promoted from Johnson City to Peoria at the end of the year; and outfielder Derek Gibson.

"Double A is the jump that everybody looks forward to," McKnight said, "but me probably more than most people. Springfield is my second home, and also for the Missouri State guys (like Voit). I've always told people the big goal is St. Louis, but my personal little goal is to get to Springfield. I remember as a senior being there and the thought never even crossed my mind that I could be there in a few years.

"My next biggest fear to getting released would be getting traded. I can't imagine playing for any other organization. Everybody in the minors has a goal of getting to the big leagues but mine goes a step farther, to play at Busch Stadium in front of all my family and friends."

Some minor-leaguers, such as Xavier Scruggs, have achieved that goal, only to see it inspire an even larger one.

25 XAVIER SCRUGGS

IT'S AN INTANGIBLE SKILL, ONE WHICH, DESPITE ALL OF THE STATISTICS
and computer analysis now available in baseball, can't be measured in any way other than by observation.

Yet its importance, especially in the success of a team and an
organization, could rank as high as any of the more quantifi-
able numbers.

"It" is the importance of being a good teammate, and as far
as Xavier Scruggs is concerned, that skill can be as valuable to a
team's performance as hitting, pitching, or fielding.

In his eight seasons in the Cardinals' minor-league system, and
some brief stretches with the major-league team, Scruggs saw
a lot of players come and go—and learned that some of those
moves had nothing to do with personal on-field failures.

The emphasis the Cardinals place on the quality of being a
good teammate, he believes, says something about the character
and the team-oriented philosophy of individuals and the role it
plays in how the team performs on the field.

"One of the biggest things I have seen is they have a way of
kind of weeding out the guys who are not going to be really

helpful in a team atmosphere," Scruggs said. "I think the No. 1 thing they think about is how guys are going to react if they make it to St. Louis.

"They are looking at guys in short-season and Single A and seeing if they are going to fit in well with a team atmosphere and not just be a 'me' guy. They want people who are not concerned just about their own statistics but people who are going to prepare themselves and be ready at the next level to be good teammates."

Nobody ever conveyed that belief to Scruggs, and he never read it in a manual. It was just obvious to him from his first days as a Cardinal, having been drafted in the 19th round in 2008 out of UNLV. The first baseman began his career at Batavia in the New York–Penn League, where the Muckdogs finished second in the regular season and then won the league championship.

There really were no future stars on that team. Six of the players on the roster have gone on to play in the major leagues, most notably Lance Lynn, the Cardinals' supplemental first-round pick in the June draft that year. Lynn began his career with six appearances in Batavia before he was quickly promoted to Quad Cities.

That team's success had more to do with their combined performances rather than individual accomplishments—and Scruggs has seen that repeated on many other teams, at every level in the organization, ever since.

"I've seen those types of guys that don't have the right attitude, who are all about themselves, and they just move them out," Scruggs said. "In some aspects you do have to be selfish in this game, but at the same time there are guys that you just know are not going to help in a team atmosphere or they are just a bad seed. They find those guys and weed them out quickly."

Beginning with that first summer in Batavia, Scruggs played nearly 900 games in the Cardinals' minor-league system, making stops on five different teams, spending most of the 2014 and 2015 seasons at Triple A Memphis. His days as a Cardinal ended in December 2015 when he signed as a minor-league free agent with the Marlins.

The 2014 and 2015 seasons also included his first exposure to the major-league team, where he appeared in a combined 26 games.

The challenge for players in Triple A, he has found, is different than at lower levels in the organization—and makes the goal of being a team-first player much more difficult. Players have to fight the distraction of seeing other players earn promotions, especially when they feel like they were more qualified, and be able to separate their personal goals from doing what they need to do to make the team successful.

"You see guys go up there when you definitely feel like you should be up there, but at the same point it's a motivating factor to know you are right there on the cusp and that the opportunity is right in front of you," Scruggs said.

One of the hardest parts of playing in Triple A is when a player has to come back down to that level after spending time in the major leagues. Scruggs has personal experience, but that doesn't make it any easier.

"You have to get re-acclimated every time, not so much to the competition but to the guys around you," he said. "Every clubhouse is different, and you just try to get comfortable as soon as possible and get back to work."

Like others who have spent time in a similar situation, Scruggs has tried to learn from his experience in the major leagues and tried to understand what it takes to be successful there.

"One of the biggest differences to me is the in-game mental focus of a player," Scruggs said. "I feel in Triple A, guys will lose focus on their job more often. It's like when a reliever comes into the game in the seventh or eighth inning. He might get the first couple of hitters out, but then he will lose focus against the next hitter and not be as sharp.

"As a hitter you have to be locked in for every at-bat, and things like your pitch recognition just have to be that much sharper. The biggest thing our coaches talk about is being mentally prepared. It's something everybody has to work on."

One of the expectations when a player goes up to the major leagues from Memphis, Scruggs said, is that he will know what is expected of him and be ready to contribute when he is called upon. Because the Cardinals have basically the same procedures for relays, cutoffs, rundowns, etc., there should be no surprises about what a player is supposed to do when he gets to the major leagues, he said.

"Everybody knows and realizes that there might be physical errors and mistakes, but they expect you to be mentally in the game and mentally aware of where you are supposed to be defensively," Scruggs said. "They expect you to know what your approach is at the plate. That way when you go from Memphis to St. Louis, nothing changes.

"You are not trying to be a different player; just do the same thing you have been doing to get that opportunity. The whole mental aspect of the game is what is really expected. A lot of guys in Triple A physically can play in St. Louis, but are they mentally ready to do what they are supposed to do? It's something you have to focus on and work on just as much as the physical part of the game."

Each player also has his own personal "to-do" list. When a player returns from St. Louis to Memphis, he usually does so with instructions from Mike Matheny and the coaching staff about what he needs to work on.

In Scruggs' individual case, he spent 2015 trying to develop a shorter swing, to have better plate discipline and pitch recognition. He also was trying to improve defensively with the chances he got to play the outfield, knowing that ability will make him more versatile than if he remained strictly a first baseman.

Scruggs' biggest success in his career has come in the area of hitting home runs. He has hit 148 in his minor-league career, including five seasons when he hit 21 or more. He has yet to hit one in the major leagues.

And that remains a motivating goal—to get that opportunity.

Now 28, Scruggs knows that his clock is ticking and he can't predict when or if his next major-league chance will come. It is something he can't control, and acknowledging that is another hard lesson that every minor-leaguer has to learn, just as was the decision to leave the Cardinals organization.

"You have to try to focus on what you can control," he said. "I feel if I do that, and do it well, things will fall in my favor.

"I want the opportunity to have a long career, but you have to think about what there is after baseball. I don't want to not be ready for the next step. Hopefully that is something which is way down the road. The one thing I have thought about is working with kids in some kind of capacity."

Scruggs, who was drafted after his junior year in college, has a couple of more classes to complete to earn his degree in sociology. Before he moves on to the next step, he wants to get that chance to hit a home run in the major leagues.

"That would mean the world to me," he said.

Scruggs is different than most of the players in the minor leagues in one respect. He already has reached the major leagues, even if he didn't stay as long as he would have liked.

One player still working to realize that dream is Carson Kelly.

26   CARSON KELLY

FOLLOWING THE COMPLETION OF HIS FIRST FULL PROFESSIONAL
season in 2013, Carson Kelly was told the Cardinals wanted
him to report to their instructional league program to get in a
few more weeks of training before the winter began.

Oh, and one other thing, said director of player development
Gary LaRocque—we want you to change positions.

Kelly had been drafted in the second round as a third baseman out of Westview High School in Portland, Oregon, in 2012,
and the Cardinals were able to lure him away from a scholarship to the University of Oregon. He played third at Johnson
City, Tennessee, that summer and in Peoria and State College,
Pennsylvania, in 2013.

"We really felt we wanted to explore this whole catching option," LaRocque said at the time he asked Kelly to make the
switch. "Carson has every quality to make this work."

Kelly, who had not caught since he was in the eighth grade,
accepted the challenge and, just two years later, already had begun to thrive at his new position.

He spent all of 2014 in Peoria, where his on-the-job training included nine errors, 13 passed balls, and throwing out 33 percent of would-be basestealers in his 79 games behind the plate. He was also selected for the Midwest League All-Star Game.

That solid season earned Kelly a promotion to high A Palm Beach in 2015, where he made an impression not only on the Cardinals with how quickly he had progressed, but throughout the minor leagues.

After the season, when he was going through the instructional league again, Kelly found out he had won the minor-league Gold Glove, awarded to only one catcher in all of the minor leagues, in only his second year behind the plate.

"I came in after batting practice and my phone was blowing up," Kelly said. "I thought, *Something must be going on*. I had no idea."

Kelly did know that all of the work and effort he had put into learning his new position had produced positive results. For the year, he committed only three errors, all on errant throws, and was charged with six passed balls in 104 games covering 920 innings. He also threw out 36 percent of runners who tried to steal against him.

"In our opinion he was the best catcher in the league," said Palm Beach manager Oliver Marmol. "He made some really nice improvements defensively. It was fun for him and good to see him make the progress."

Once Kelly agreed to change positions, he knew the only chance he had to make it a successful move was to 100 percent buy in to the idea and to work hard at everything he needed to learn.

It definitely helped that one of his instructors in spring training in 2014, when he was a non-roster invite to the Cardinals' big-league camp, was Yadier Molina.

Molina welcomes the chance to work with young catchers every spring, beating them to the team's facility every morning and meeting them in the batting cages before the sun comes up.

Kelly, a good student in school as well as on the baseball field, was exactly the kind of pupil Molina enjoys.

"He's a good kid," said Molina, knowing Kelly was still only 19 years old. "It's like when I was a kid like him, doing the same thing with Mike Matheny. I do like it, because this kid is a good listener. He wants to get better each day and he works hard… He's going to be good."

The workout day for the team's catchers is usually longer than that of any other players during the spring, but Kelly's education extended even after he left the ballpark. He went back to his hotel room, pulled out a pad of paper, and wrote down notes about what he had learned that day.

"I usually pick up stuff pretty quickly," he said that spring. "I like to write stuff down so I can go back and refer to it. I keep daily notes on the pitchers I've caught and what they throw. I do it after practice. It's helped me and kind of gets the learning curve growing a little bit."

That education has continued the last two seasons, and included more classes in Molina's school in the spring of 2015. As much as he has learned, and as hard as he has worked, Kelly realizes that his education continues every day he finds himself behind the plate.

"Winning (the Gold Glove) within two years is really a blessing," he said. "It makes me more motivated to keep going and get better."

While Kelly's first instruction included the fundamental skills of catching the ball, blocking balls in the dirt, and how to position himself for throws, concentrating on his footwork, he has now advanced to the more cerebral parts of learning the ins and outs of the position.

And that is probably the side of catching that Kelly enjoys the most, because not only is he a student of the game, he is a real student as well, continuing his education while playing in the minor leagues through online classes from Oregon State.

Kelly is majoring in economics and regularly takes classes during spring training, the regular season, and even when he is in the instructional league. In October 2015 he had just started his fall semester of three classes—physics, evolution, and environmental sustainability.

"I'm getting to the point where I have to take the hard classes," he said. "The hardest class I've had was differential calculus. I didn't do great in that class because it is the hardest one to teach yourself, which is basically what I am doing. I have about two years of classes left before I will have my degree."

When he was drafted by the Cardinals, continuing his education was something Kelly knew he would do, whether he turned down the offer to go pro or signed. He believes that the combination of playing baseball and taking the online classes has worked well.

"In high school I actually played a lot better when I had the most stressful time in school, which I know sounds kind of weird," Kelly said. "It just keeps your brain moving. Continuing to go to school gets your brain going a lot more than sitting around watching television."

Kelly has talked to some of his minor-league teammates about pursuing their degrees through on-line classes. Some of them are even looking into going on to graduate school if they have already earned their degree.

"You've always got to have a backup plan," Kelly said. "This game is a tough game and you never know what's going to happen. A lot of guys get out of baseball and then they don't know what to do. Having that degree allows you to do what you want to do. I know it's a really small percentage of major-league players who actually have their college degree, and that's something to take pride in. It's something inside me that is really important."

Being a good student, both with his transition to catching and in his academic work, made Kelly very aware that one of the toughest parts of changing positions was the element of time management. Putting in so much time working to develop his skills as a catcher did have a cost attached to it—a lack of time to work on the offensive part of the game.

It showed when he hit just .180 over the first three months of the 2015 season, with three homers and 27 RBIs. The Florida State League, where teams play in the same stadiums used by the major-league teams in spring training, always makes it tough to put up big offensive numbers, but Kelly knew he was a better hitter than those statistics reflected.

He showed that in the last three months of the year, when he hit .268 with five homers and 24 RBIs.

"He was very impressive in the second half," Marmol said. "He put together some very quality at-bats. Things started to click for him and you could tell the game started to slow down a little bit. He was using the whole field, and you could just tell he was more comfortable.

"The organization kind of knew that part of his offensive struggles were because of the change in positions. He put in a lot of time becoming a good catcher but it was good to see the offense start to click as well."

Kelly actually believes that not doing as well as he would have liked offensively made him work even harder to become a better catcher.

"It kind of took a toll on me a little bit," he said about not hitting well. "But when you're not hitting you go and do everything you can to help your team defensively. Some of the times when I didn't hit the greatest was when I actually caught my best. When you're not doing as well as you want in one aspect of the game, you try to make the other side that much better.

"In the second half I was able to focus more on the mental side of catching and that allowed me to focus more on my hitting. The priority always was to be a good catcher, and still is, but when you are doing better offensively you have a better attitude and it makes everything a lot easier."

As happy as he is to be a Cardinal, and with his decision to sign coming out of high school, Kelly was not surprised that his brother, Parker, a right-handed pitcher, made the opposite decision in 2015 after he was drafted by the Cardinals. He turned down the team's offer and went to school at Oregon.

The Cardinals will have another chance to draft Parker in three years, and, then, he might have a chance to throw to his brother.

"It's a process," Kelly said. "I've got to continue to keep learning and developing. I've only been at this a few years, even though it feels like I've been here a long time. You've got to keep working because there is always somebody wanting to take your job."

And if Kelly ever needs a reminder to remain humble, he only has to think back a couple of years, to spring training in

2013. He was in his first minor-league camp when he was called over to be a late-inning sub in the major-league Cardinals' game against the Marlins.

As he took his position at third base in the sixth inning, he heard the stadium's public address announcer say, "Now playing third base, Joe Kelly."

"I was like, *Wait, I'm not Joe Kelly*," he said. "The funny thing is I was sitting next to Joe in the dugout before I went out there."

If the Cardinals' projections for Kelly are correct, that mistake likely won't ever happen again.

One person who clearly believes that is Marmol, his manager not only at Palm Beach but in 2013 at State College as well.

27   OLIVER MARMOL

EVEN THOUGH JUPITER, FLORIDA, IS MORE THAN 1,100 MILES AND three levels from St. Louis, there is perhaps no team in the Cardinals' farm system more connected to the major-league team than the Class A Palm Beach Cardinals.

The team uses the same clubhouse, the same weight room, the same training facilities, and the same batting cages that the major-league players occupy during spring training. The team even plays its home games in the same stadium.

Just outside the door of the clubhouse is manager Oliver Marmol's office, the same one occupied by Cardinals manager Mike Matheny for six weeks in February and March.

That connection, Marmol believes, carries an important message about how the organization truly is one large family.

"You hear that this is a 'family' all the time, and I truly believe it is true here," Marmol said. "There is a close relationship between all of the staff members. This is a small complex, and when the major-league team is here, the minor-league people are right down the hall. You can't really hide from anybody.

"That closeness between everybody makes it fun to come to

work. We can have disagreements but we speak freely and respectfully and we work it out and come to the best conclusion. I think that's part of what makes us good."

Sometimes the conversations a manager has with a player in the office are difficult, and no one knows that better than Marmol. He has been on both sides of the desk in this office.

Marmol was a 23-year-old infielder on the Palm Beach Cardinals in 2010 when he was called into the office and informed that he was being released.

The news wasn't really a surprise to Marmol, who had been drafted by the Cardinals in the sixth round of the 2007 draft out of the College of Charleston in South Carolina but had not really progressed the way either he or the organization had hoped.

During his four years, Marmol never hit better than .221 and never played a game above A ball. The Cardinals saw skills beyond his playing ability, however, and offered him a chance to stay in the organization. He served as the hitting coach for the Gulf Coast League Cardinals in 2011 and then became the manager of rookie-level Johnson City in 2012.

Marmol moved up to State College, Pennsylvania, in the New York–Penn League in 2013 and spent two years managing the Spikes, winning the league title in 2014, before he was promoted to Palm Beach for the 2015 season.

"In my head, even when I was in college, I knew I wanted to someday coach and lead other men," Marmol said. "*When* was the question—how long could I play this game? When that decision was made for me, it was a really easy transition. I never had an itch to play again. Maybe I just didn't miss hitting .220, but I never had an itch to get back on the field and play the game.

"I can honestly say I enjoy leading these guys from a managing standpoint much more than I did playing. It's not even close."

Perhaps it is because of his background as a player that Marmol has become an effective leader at a young age—he was just 25 when he began managing in Johnson City, at the time the youngest manager in affiliated ball in the minor leagues—but those skills also can be traced back even further, to when he was growing up, and learned the importance of helping others from his parents.

"I grew up always seeing my parents being very giving," he said. "They were always very lending of their time and resources, so I saw that as kind of a norm."

Marmol's family was living in Miami in the summer of 1992, the year he turned six, when Hurricane Andrew struck south Florida, destroying at least 800 homes. One of them belonged to his family.

"We had absolutely nothing," Marmol said. "I remember pretty vividly how people came along to help us. Seeing how people gave their time and money, food and resources, everything, had a lasting impact on me."

When he was a junior in high school, after the family had moved to Orlando, Marmol began going to church—and learned another lesson in the importance of helping others before yourself. That is still something he is doing now, and in bigger and more meaningful ways than he likely thought possible.

The minister of his church in Palm Beach first approached Marmol and his wife, Amber, a few years ago about going to visit an orphanage run by the minister's daughter in Guatemala. The couple agreed and went there in February 2011.

"That trip opened my eyes completely to what else is out there," Marmol said. "I saw all of the needs and some of the things we could help with immediately."

The Marmols saw that the mission of the orphanage was to try to teach children a trade so they might be able to support themselves once they reached adulthood.

"When Amber and I got back we started talking about how we could do something that would have some longevity and have some sustained giving," he said. "We saw ways we could help."

The Marmols created a company offering batting lessons and baseball instruction. They decided half of the money earned through the company would be given away.

"The first year we were able to give money to help a village in Haiti," Marmol said. "They sent us a picture of a big wooden table with probably 20 kids sitting around it. They had been eating one meal maybe every three days or so. For six months after our donation they were eating two or three meals a day."

Their donations included building a chicken farm and providing the chickens, another way of ensuring the children in the village would have something to eat.

"It was cool to see that immediate return," Marmol said. "We are now trying to partner with other people and find ways to do more. I couldn't care less who gets the credit. At the end of the day it's 'Are these kids eating? Are they getting an education? Are they being led spiritually and in the right direction?'"

The Marmols became friends with the founders of Hope Project International, and they were approached in 2014 about taking a "baseball" mission trip to Nicaragua.

"They asked me if I could get a couple of players to take that trip," he said. "We got it going kind of on the spur of the moment.

Three players who were on the State College team—Nick Thompson, Collin Radack, and Jeff Rauh—agreed to go with us."

What they saw on the trip to Cristo Rey in November 2014 was even more powerful than what Marmol and his wife had observed the previous year during their visit to the orphanage in Guatamala.

"The poverty we saw really opened our eyes, the way those kids were living," he said. "They were poking through trash. There literally was nothing but trash up to your knees for as far as you could see. There was nothing there."

Marmol said the group saw children following dump trucks filled with trash, hoping they could be the first to find something they could eat when the trucks emptied their load.

"We were in a minivan and when we turned the corner, that was literally all we could see," Marmol said. "That's how life happens there."

Radack had been to Nicaragua before, but had never seen anything like what he experienced on this trip.

"When I was a freshman in college I went with my church group," Radack said. "We went and built a house and did some stuff with a school. We stayed in Managua.

"We were definitely in a poorer community on this trip. They lived in a trash dump."

The group spent its first two days in Nicaragua rebuilding a house for a family where the children had to hide under a staircase when it rained because of a leaking roof. In addition to trying to stay dry, they were worried the roof would collapse.

They also visited an orphanage in the area, learning more about what they could do to help and perhaps provide some hope and evoke some smiles from the children.

The answer, as Marmol expected would be the case, was baseball.

Marmol and the players had brought a lot of baseball equipment with them. For children who had used sticks for bats, socks wrapped around marbles for balls, and tree stumps for bases, being able to use real bats, balls, and gloves did indeed bring the smiles that Marmol and the players in his group had hoped to see. The next day, when more children showed up, Marmol and his players divided everyone into two teams and played an actual game.

Marmol did not forget about those children when he returned to Florida. He went to work trying to raise more money, planning for another trip.

Marmol planned to go back to Nicaragua after the 2015 season to lay the groundwork for the construction of a two-floor building that would include a kitchen and a computer lab.

"We want to see them learn how to cook and learn a trade," Marmol said. "We want to get an idea of the costs and what the building will look like, and hopefully can start the project sooner rather than later."

The next stage of the project will hopefully include the development of a baseball field.

"It would be really cool to offer those kids an outlet of baseball, something they could have fun doing," Marmol said. "We're trying to find the funding for it, then a lot of it already is a go. We want people to come on board and see the overall picture of what we are trying to do."

Marmol is hopeful there will be a way that he can connect baseball to getting the kids going to school on a regular basis, beginning to provide an education for children where one is often not available. Access to medical care could follow.

"It's just the beginning of something that can be pretty neat," he said. "I'd like to go back and start building some of that. We're getting some of the layouts of the buildings and the projected costs together. We're starting to take a better look at how we can get the project moving."

The Marmols also have stayed in touch with the children they met at the orphanage in Guatemala more than five years ago. Those trips have forever changed their lives.

"When we got back, a comment was made to my wife and me that (the trip) had shown us how blessed we are," Marmol said. "Not that it rubbed me the wrong way, but the big picture is, yes, we are blessed but now let's do something about it. We do have a lot—even when we think we don't, we do.

"It gives you a perspective not so much on what we have but how we can truly make an impact, and it's not hard. When people come together and don't care about who gets the credit you can accomplish a heck of a lot. You can make a difference in those people's lives."

The parallel to his job as a minor-league manager, even if not in a financial sense, is obvious.

"It does give you an interesting perspective about what it is we do here," Marmol said, sitting in the chair behind his desk in the concrete-walled office. "It doesn't change my outlook on the importance of what we do here. The truth is it actually makes me want to do this job that much better. The better we are at what we do in our jobs the greater impact we can continue to have outside of here.

"My job when I get here is to plan how I can make an impact on the lives that are in that clubhouse and lead them to be men that know how to lead others—to understand their careers are important and provide them the ability to have an impact out there. This job is extremely important."

As a manager, even now at the age of 29, Marmol is only a few years older than the players he is directing. When he was in State College in 2013, he actually was younger than one of his players, returning Navy Lt. Mitch Harris.

Away from the field, however, Marmol is usually drawn to people older than himself—for a reason.

"Growing up I had three older brothers," Marmol said. "My wife one time asked me why most of my friends were older. I always found it interesting to look at other people's lives and learn from them.

"A lot of things I learned came from my brothers. There were a lot of things I learned not to do, just observing what works and what doesn't work and how to implement it in my own life. I don't talk much. I do a lot of observing, figuring out the best ways to go about doing things, whether in life or just in this job."

While much of what he learned about managing came while watching and observing during his playing career, Marmol also has sought out advice from others in the Cardinals organization, such as Mike Shildt, Mark DeJohn, Gary LaRocque, and Mike Matheny.

"Really the biggest lesson I have learned about this job is that you are managing people," Marmol said. "That's the most important thing—caring about them as people and not as players. I've learned that's what gets you results, how you get people to play really hard for you. They have to know you care about them."

Marmol never had the chance to meet George Kissell but he knows the legacy—and is continuing to put Kissell's philosophy into action.

"You have to learn if they have kids, you have to know about their wives," he said. "That's important. The baseball stuff is different. They are natural competitors and they are all going to compete to get better on the field. That's a given. Let's care about them as people and get them to understand this is a family and we're going to go in this direction."

Marmol got a firsthand lesson in the importance of relationships during his time in State College, when he and his players met a special 10-year-old named Josiah Viera.

The youngster first became associated with the team when it was a Pirates affiliate, through the Children's Miracle Network. He came to a couple of games in 2013, getting to know Marmol, the coaches, and some of the players, and was at almost every home game in 2014.

Josiah was only a few months old when his family learned he was suffering from a rare medical condition known as Hutchinson-Gilford progeria, which causes premature aging in children.

"He's gone through a lot and fought through a lot, more than anything we've ever fought through," Marmol said. "He brings joy to the field every day. He thinks we're doing something for him but he did a tremendous job of bringing life to that clubhouse and putting everything in perspective.

"It was definitely an inspiration to have him in the clubhouse and around the guys and just being part of the group. The guys loved having him around."

The Spikes gave Josiah his own locker in the clubhouse, and uniform No. 10, and he participated in the pregame drills, batting practice, and the exchange of lineup cards before games, which he took in from the dugout. All the while, Josiah kept reminding the team of his goal for the season.

"From the very beginning he said he wanted a championship," Marmol said.

The Spikes honored Josiah's wishes by winning the New York–Penn League title, and Josiah was there to join in the postgame celebration.

"It was special for him to be there for it and for us to pull it off," Marmol said. "It definitely was an added bonus."

Josiah's grandfather drove him to Troy, New York, so he could be there for the final game of the championship series against the Tri-City Valley Cats, an Astros farm club.

He was cheering as the Spikes exploded for six runs in the first inning and went on to the 11–2 victory.

"It was like something out of a movie, honestly, it worked out perfectly," said outfielder Chase Raffield. "It worked out the way God wanted it to. He blessed us with a championship, and to have Josiah be a part of it. It was amazing.

"That last game, we were playing to win, but we were playing more to win it for him. I think that was what was on everybody's mind."

After the final out, Josiah didn't hesitate. He knew exactly what to do.

"He went nuts," Marmol said. "He went crazy. He sprinted toward the field, the guys picked him up and made sure it was a moment he could enjoy. He was very excited, just yelling and running around. The guys were having a good time with him. It definitely was a day he's not going to forget."

Marmol credited Josiah for providing an extra incentive for the team, as did his players, who got another lesson in the perspective about life and not just baseball that Marmol values so much.

"It's not very often that you find someone that can impact your life so much," said pitcher Trey Nielsen. "Everyone loved that kid. He was part of the family. He's one of the smartest kids I've ever met. It's something you don't anticipate when you hear his story, what he has and what he's been through. You don't expect a kid like that to have that knowledge.

"He knows so much about the game, and he loves the game. Honestly if you are going to say one thing about him, it's that he taught us to love the game through how much he loves it. He has the true passion that everyone speaks of. He found a connection with people through baseball and so did we. He honestly became one of my best friends."

Added Raffield, "I can't really tell you who benefitted the most or had the better experience, us or Josiah. For me being a part of it, it was such a blessing to be around him. I gained so much from that kid, seeing his heart and love for the game. He was always happy. That was something we all took away from it. He gave everybody a better attitude.

"God puts things in our hearts and makes everybody different, and I think He made Josiah to love baseball. Josiah touched so many lives…He's intense. He will pick up on so many things and other guys might not. He's so intelligent and so clued in to the game. 'You need to run out that ground ball,' he would say, or he would walk up to you and say, 'Suck it up, man.' What do you say to that? 'You're right, OK,' and then keep on going. He made it a really light clubhouse, but kept us focused on what really mattered."

Marmol hopes he never loses that perspective. He had it in Palm Beach in 2015, when he directed his team to the South Division second-half title and a trip to the Florida State League playoffs.

It was a trip he knows was years in the making, and was a result of all the help and advice he received along the way.

"DeJohn helped me with in-game stuff. Shildt also had a huge role in that," Marmol said. "They poured a lot of knowledge into me about how to prepare for games. They were very intentional in how they went about teaching me.

"When I got the Johnson City job, I was so much trying to figure out what I was doing I didn't have time to think if I was ready or not. I was just trying to learn as I went. I'm pretty comfortable with not knowing things. I'm OK with that. It doesn't bother me to not have answers to things, so I ask questions. I'm comfortable doing that.

"It was never, 'Am I ready for this?' It was, 'How quickly can I learn?' I never doubted myself. I've always had good people around me who I could ask questions and learn as I went and not be afraid to make a mistake."

What Marmol, in essence, was learning and then learning to pass along to others was the Cardinal way.

"It comes with a ton of accountability from the very top of the organization to the bottom," he said. "There is just that sense of accountability. Expectations are high. If I do something that is not going to make us better today then I will be called out on it. That's how it's supposed to be. You can't get by with doing things that don't work. You are held to a higher standard and everybody understands that.

"That's the fun part about showing up for work. You've got to be ready. Somebody will call you out if you're not, and that's a beautiful thing. You can't just half-ass it."

Because he is so young, it would be easy for Marmol to wonder about his future, where he might one day be in the game, and how much his mission work outside of baseball can accomplish.

If he has long-term goals, however, Marmol is not willing to share them. It is one of his strengths, the ability to focus on what he can control, that has made him successful in baseball and in life.

He is not willing to gaze very far into the future.

"As I sit here I see that I have a game at 6:35 tonight and I have to figure out a way to get those guys going," he said of his players. "I get this question (about his future) quite often, and I don't entertain it. I really don't.

"At the end of the season when Gary (LaRocque) pulls me into the office and tells me what my assignment is for next year, I will nod my head and go back to work. I have no real goals about five years from now; I just want to do my job well.

"I knew early on that at some point I would like to lead guys from the seat of managing, but as far as an end game, I have no answer. I've never thought of it long enough to have an answer."

Marmol really has the same answer to the question of what he wants to accomplish through his mission work in Haiti, Guatemala, Nicaragua, and other countries he has yet to visit. The Dominican Republic and India are future possibilities. His brother, the missions pastor at a church in South Carolina, was organizing those trips.

"The truth is I can plan all I want and it's great, but God is going to take it in any direction He wants," Marmol said. "The truth is it's already going in that direction. I never saw it going. It's already bigger than I ever imaged it being.

"A long-term vision? Keep feeding kids, that's about it. It's going to be cool to see where it leads. I have no idea where it's going but we are completely open to anything and everything that can help those kids—help them get an education, help them get fed, and see where it goes from there. I am really excited about some of the opportunities."

The Marmols hope one day to start a family of their own, but they will never forget all of the other children who have touched their lives.

"Unless you have the chance to leave here and go to these countries, you don't even know it exists," he said. "You come back and figure out how we can change that. You think if it is happening all over the world, what a difference that is going to make. It makes a huge difference.

"When you sit with a little girl who is crying because when it rains it just pours on her bed and you've just built the family a house, that's neat. It's not going to rain on her anymore. You see kids who don't have food, and for the next six months they are eating three meals a day—you know you did something.

"Whether it's for a village of 20 kids or 200 kids, it's irrelevant. Twenty kids are now eating, or 200 kids are now eating. That's the way I look at it."

28   STEVE TURCO

STEVE TURCO IS A PATIENT MAN. YOU CAN'T BE A MANAGER IN ROOKIE ball for 14 years, where players make frequent mistakes, and not be.

"There's a reason why there are erasers on pencils," he said. "Everybody makes mistakes."

It is those mistakes, by some of the youngest players in the Cardinals' farm system, which Turco uses as teaching points as the manager of the Gulf Coast League Cardinals, a job he has had for the last seven years.

"I think you learn more from your mistakes," Turco said. "You gain confidence from your successes, but the way you learn is to make a mistake and try not to do it again."

Most of the players on Turco's roster are in their first season as professionals or, in the case of the international players, at least their first year playing in the United States. There is more involved to that transition, from high school or college to the pros, or to living in a foreign country, than strictly being able to hit a curveball or throw a slider for strikes.

Turco's task is laying the foundation of what it is like to be a Cardinal.

"The emphasis of my job is to teach them about how to be a professional," Turco said. "There are mechanical things we talk about on the field, as far as technique and the rules they need to follow, but I think it's more about how to have a plan and do things the right way.

"I've been with the Cardinals a long time. And I think we do have a special organization. The Cardinal way, to me, in a nutshell is quality of character and doing things the right way. We take pride in doing things the right way, with attention to detail, but before you can do that I think you have to grasp concepts. Once you've done that, then you can refine more detail-oriented items."

Turco played in the Cardinals system from 1979 to 1984. He spent five of those six years in A ball, playing both the infield and outfield, before transitioning to coaching.

He spent a couple of years in the organization, then left to become a high school coach. Turco returned to the Cardinals as a coach in 1991, and in 1993 was named manager of Glens Falls in the New York-Penn League. Turco moved to Johnson City the following season and stayed with the Appalachian League team for six years before becoming a scout for the organization.

After working in that capacity for nine years, Turco again put on a uniform in 2009 and has been in charge of the GCL Cardinals ever since. He was named the winner of the Kissell Award in 2011 in recognition of his accomplishments in player development.

One of the daily challenges of Turco's job is to get players ready to play at noon under a hot Florida summer sun on a back field. There is no glamour in this league, virtually no fans, and no scoreboard to keep track of the game.

"It's difficult to get motivated," Turco said. "You had better be inwardly motivated and inwardly focused. I try to keep it upbeat and keep my energy level higher so hopefully they will feed off what I'm doing. Even when we get our butts kicked we are going to fight to the end.

"There are no fans to make you feel bad about a bad play—and that's a blessing at times, but it's also hard. Guys that repeat this league certainly don't want to be here again once they've been through it and know what it's like.

"The weather can be sweltering at times and stifling sometimes when the only breeze you get is when you move around and create your own. We try to tell the players it's your career and it should be more important to you than it is to us. What you are willing to put into it is what you are going to get out of it."

The lack of fans helps ease some of the pressure on the players, Turco believes, and makes it easier for this level to be almost exclusively a teaching league.

"We don't have fans who are going to be upset based on the way we play, and that's one of the good things about the GCL," he said. "While we don't want to lose, we have less at stake, so we can afford to do some things."

Many of the lessons that Turco tries to pass along to his players were ones he learned firsthand from George Kissell during both his playing days in the organization and his first few years as a young manager.

Turco is one of the people still with the Cardinals with a direct link to Kissell, and he knows his players benefit from that connection even though they never had the privilege of meeting him.

"We still mention his name," Turco said. "It hits my lips daily when we are talking about baseball and some of the things he said. We call them Kissellisms. Guys who were around him for years still talk about him like he was here today.

"He was a teacher. I learned to love the man early on. Everything he said just captivated you. Guys like him, Hub Kittle, Bo Milliken, and Dave Ricketts were the ones who were always around when I was growing up through the system. George and Hub had bigger-than-life personalities. I listened to everything they said so intently. You hung on every word George said. Everything he shared with us as players was everything I ever shared with other players.

"I have some of my own thoughts about the game, but they were shaped by things I learned from him. I haven't deviated to this day. When you are down two or three runs, take a strike. If you are down one or four, you're swinging. That was George Kissell's philosophy."

When it comes to working with the young pitchers, including many high draft picks, Turco still believes in another Kissell philosophy.

"What we emphasize here is fastball command," he said. "We want to see their off-speed stuff, we want to see that growth. But when they leave here we want to see the fastball command.

"The guys who are still around here who spent a lot of time with George pass along that knowledge. Our players now reap the rewards of that. Talking about him is really almost the same as having him here. He was a motivator. He was able to go ahead and criticize you with a strong tongue-lashing, but before he left you he would build you up. He never left you down. He would get his message across but never left you feeling bad when he left."

Turco never would have imagined that more than 20 years after he first became a minor-league manager, so much of what he says and does could be traced back to Kissell.

"Some of the things he did and said when I was a young manager wouldn't have worked at all for me," he said. "He had so much time and experience and credibility. When Ted Simmons was the farm director, he told us we weren't allowed to have hunches as young coaches. Guys like George had hunches based on experience.

"If we said we had a hunch (Simmons) would get furious. We had to have a sound reason for why we did what we did. Once you have that experience of going through tough times and going through a situation, then you are able to say 'I've got a hunch.' George would always tell us to have reasons for why you do what you do, and if you have reasons, nobody should be able to second-guess you.

"His philosophy with managers was that nobody should come into another man's house and rearrange the furniture. You know your team better than anybody."

One of the lessons which Turco remembers, and tries to pass along to his players, is that there is more than one way to do something.

"George would never tell you that, and Ricketts was the same way," Turco said. "If you had success he wouldn't care how you did it. They just wanted to see that success. These guys were incredible teachers, George probably being the best I've ever been around. I would put George up against anybody."

While Turco enjoys the challenge of working with young players, it is not an easy job. In the 2015 season, he had one player quit and go home after just three days, deciding the baseball life just wasn't what he thought it would be. Turco tried to get him to give the decision more time to no avail.

He had another player walk into his office complaining about a lost pair of sunglasses. He also watched Max Foody, a promising left-handed pitcher, make the difficult decision to retire, for a second time, because of arm injuries, not wanting to go through all of the rehab necessary following Tommy John surgery.

The Cardinals are particularly careful with the workload for their young pitchers, knowing they have already spent a high school or college season before reporting to Jupiter. Instruction and adapting to the professional life are more important than wins at this level.

Turco's title is manager, but his job involves much more responsibility than that.

"You wear a lot of hats here," he said. "Getting the players to listen, as a teacher, you just have to repeat, repeat, repeat. I tell them my job first and foremost is to help you understand how to be a professional. I am teaching you about the game, but that's almost secondary.

"If you get to St. Louis and you are not a true professional, you won't stay. This is an easy sell for us. The organization from the top all the way down is filled with men who have character. When you are that way at the top, it permeates down through the organization. We've had a lot of success. There has to be some merit to it."

One player who got a chance to experience that success in 2015, even when it really was unexpected, was Travis Tartamella.

29   TRAVIS TARTAMELLA

FOR MOST OF THE 200-PLUS PLAYERS IN THE CARDINALS' MINOR-
league system in any given year, their hopes of one day playing
in the major leagues will never be realized.

They keep grinding, however, never abandoning that dream
of one day getting the call that will change their lives. And
if those players ever need an example of why they should
never give up hope, they will always be able to look to Travis
Tartamella.

Tartamella was the 19th-round pick of the Cardinals in the
2009 draft out of Cal State–Los Angeles. His name was never
included in a list of the organization's top prospects. He never
was discussed as a future major-leaguer. In seven minor-league
seasons from 2009 through 2015, only once was his batting average higher than .226.

Tartamella, however, might be one of the keys to the success
of the Cardinals.

When it came time for one of the organization's top pitching
prospects to step onto the mound the last few years, they found
Tartamella waiting for them behind the plate.

Carlos Martinez, Trevor Rosenthal, and Kevin Siegrist all worked with Tartamella on their road to St. Louis. So too did Tim Cooney, Marco Gonzales, and Tyler Lyons in 2015. It was not a coincidence.

Mike Shildt has managed Tartamella in Johnson City, Springfield, and Memphis, and he knows that whenever he needed an assignment carried out, all he had to do was give the information to Tartamella.

"He's a guy you can count on, who goes about it the right way," Shildt said. "He's going to give you everything he's got, for the right reasons. It wasn't a stretch early on to identify his positive traits."

When the Cardinals wanted Martinez to throw more fast-balls during his starts at Double A, Tartamella got it done, and that's only one of many examples.

"He's basically like our Yadi (Molina)," Springfield pitcher Kurt Heyer said of Tartamella in a 2014 interview with the *Springfield News-Leader*. "He's got that leadership role."

Tartamella, as might be expected, gets uncomfortable when praised and is quick to give credit to the pitchers.

"I've been fortunate to catch some of the very talented pitchers coming up through the system," he said. "They are so talented they don't need a guy like me to make them better. Mike (Shildt) gave me an opportunity to catch them and try to help them out with anything I could see."

Part of what Tartamella has learned about catching over the years, to no one's surprise, has come from Molina. Molina makes it a point to work with all of the organization's young catchers during spring training.

Tartamella has been a non-roster invite to the big-league

camp twice, and each time has valued the time, and lessons, he got from Molina.

"There's so much pride in all of our catchers in the organization, and it has to start with him and Mike Matheny," Tartamella said. "When you watch all of the technical stuff he does, it's mind-boggling. Just watching how he goes about his job has been the biggest thing to help me.

"He's taught me so much in those workouts. He's the best of the best and you just try to soak in anything he has to offer. Just look at how he goes about his business. It's not something he talks about but we just watch him and see how professional he is. He's always working hard and striving to get better. It's no coincidence that he's the best in the business."

In turn, the knowledge that Molina has passed on to Tartamella—as Dave Ricketts and Matheny passed on to Molina when he was a young catcher years ago—has given Tartamella the ability to help others. The Cardinals don't make it a secret that they put a lot of responsibility in the hands of their catchers and the role they play in the success of their pitchers and the overall team and organization.

It's one of the philosophies of the organization, and really no different than watching Jon Jay working with young outfielders in the spring, offering advice and suggestions to a player who he knows in his heart could one day take his job on the major-league roster.

The selflessness, the ability to put team above individual, is a spirit and a togetherness that Matheny has embraced and encouraged since becoming the Cardinals' manager in 2012. That is something not every team can claim, but it truly is one of the differences in the Cardinals, and one of the reasons for their success.

When he signed, of course, Tartamella was like every other young minor-leaguer who thought his future would include time in the big leagues.

A former football player, Tartamella believes his success in that sport was what led him to want to become a catcher.

"I thought I was better at football, but once I got out there and put the pads on and started getting hit around, I really wanted to become a catcher," he said. "It's kind of my niche."

Tartamella believes he has gotten better over the years as he has gained more experience.

"When I first got into the system I know people thought I blocked the ball well and caught well," he said. "Seven years later I also take pride in my game management and helping out the pitchers and working the game. That's something you only learn in time."

Another lesson that is not quickly learned is to appreciate the value of a player like Tartamella, even though that value is not always measured in statistics or a box score. A career .197 hitter in 996 minor-league at-bats—Tartamella's numbers—would not, on paper, stand out as being very impressive or those of a future major-leaguer.

The game of baseball, however, is not played on paper.

"It's all process driven," Tartamella said. "That's the way the Cardinals go about it. It takes more time for some, less for others, to find out what process is going to help them become successful. As long as you have a solid foundation and stick with it, you're going to be successful.

"Starting from a young age, the Cardinals stress the importance of fundamentals. They put a big emphasis on that and on being professional. I think that goes a long way and kind of weeds out some people who maybe are not good fits for the organization.

"My mom and dad were very hard-working people and they instilled that in me. I always try to do everything to the best of my ability and go from there.

"My role is to be a good teammate, catch bullpens, and help guys out. I'm thankful to be a Cardinal. I'm really blessed to be a part of the organization. I can't complain about anything."

Tartamella watched a lot of his teammates in Memphis move on to St. Louis during the 2015 season, where they got a chance to contribute to the major-league team's success.

"You get a lot of joy out of watching your teammates," he said. "It's a thrill to turn on the television and see them."

Tartamella thought his 2015 season had ended when Memphis played its final regular-season game on September 7. Two weeks later he was at his grandmother's house in California when his plans changed.

Molina suffered a torn ligament in his left thumb in a game in Chicago on September 20, an injury which forced him to miss the rest of the regular season. Needing catching insurance, the Cardinals reached out to Tartamella and told him he was being called up.

Three days later, at the age of 27, he made his major-league debut, coming in to catch the final two innings of a 10–2 win over the Cincinnati Reds. He came to bat in the bottom of the eighth. Later admitting that his hands were shaking, Tartamella swung at the first pitch from Carlos Contreras and singled to right field.

Standing on first base, as the ball was thrown into the dugout for safekeeping, Tartamella knew everything he had gone through for seven years was worth it to experience that one moment.

The Cardinals, and Matheny in particular, were happy to give him that chance.

"He's a good resource for us," Matheny said. "The team was so excited for him. He's just been the epitome of a grinder. You talk to pitchers, which I do, when they come up and you ask, 'What was going on down there, what was working well for you, who really invested in you?' Consistently they say, 'Travis,' and they say how he would take so much pride in doing the little things right behind the plate.

"To watch him walk out there, I mean, I had goosebumps. I'm not lying…and then to get a hit? That's all storybook stuff."

It's also the story of the Cardinals, and how they have built the best franchise in baseball.

ACKNOWLEDGMENTS

THE AUTHOR WISHES TO THANK ALL OF THE PEOPLE WHO HELPED IN the writing and production of this book. Special thanks go out to the media relations directors of the Cardinals' minor-league affiliates, who assisted with interview requests, photos, and much more: Michael Whitty of the Memphis Redbirds, Andrew Buchbinder of the Springfield Cardinals, Nathan Baliva of the Peoria Chiefs, and Joe Putnam of the State College Spikes. Thanks also to Cardinals general manager John Mozeliak and director of player development Gary LaRocque for their assistance, and to Adam Motin and Tom Bast at Triumph Books for believing in the project.